The Merchant of Venice

The Merchant of Venice

As Directed by
Mark Lamos

Edited by
Elliott Hayes
and
Michal Schonberg

Costume Sketches by
Christina Poddubiuk

CBC Enterprises

MONTRÉAL • TORONTO • NEW YORK • LONDON

Published by CBC Enterprises, a division of the Canadian Broadcasting Corporation, Box 500,
Station A, Toronto (Ontario), Canada M5W 1E6, in association with The Stratford
Shakespearean Festival Foundation of Canada, Box 520, Stratford (Ontario), Canada N5A 6V2.

The Artistic Director of The Stratford Shakespearean Festival is John Hirsch.

CANADIAN CATALOGUING IN PUBLICATION DATA

Shakespeare, William, 1564-1616.
    The merchant of Venice

Stratford Festival ed.
ISBN 0-88794-130-3

I. CBC Enterprises.   II. Title.

PR2825.A1 1984   822.3'3   C84-098522-3

Publisher: Glenn Edward Witmer
Editor: Betty Corson
Design: Leslie Smart and Associates Limited
Layout and Assembly: First Image
Typesetter: Video Text Incorporated
Printer: D.W. Friesen and Sons Limited

Printed and bound in Canada

1 2 3 4 5 6 7 / 91 90 89 88 87 86 85

Contents

Illuminating
The Merchant of Venice by the Light
of Renaissance Christianity
by Mark Lamos

*T*he Merchant of Venice strikes me as a play that examines ideas most of us
would prefer not to face. Because Shakespeare delineates the
characters and actions with a sense of divinely omniscient irony, the
audience is placed in an ambiguous, shifting, and uncomfortable position. We
are on *terra infirma*, forced to think about what we watch and judge our
reactions with self-critical awareness. The play's shifting ironies, mercurial
changes, and its effects of self-parody and self-examination are the qualities
that make *The Merchant of Venice* so disturbingly unique – and it is precisely
these qualities that link the play to an important Renaissance religious
holiday called Shrovetide. By understanding the themes of this holiday, we
can begin to approach the play's central ironies.

Although *The Merchant of Venice* probably premièred in 1596 or 1597, the
first recorded account of a performance was at the court of James I on Shrove
Sunday, February 10, 1605. The King commanded a second performance to
be staged two days later on Shrove Tuesday, which immediately precedes
Ash Wednesday, the first day of Lent. The fact that *The Merchant of Venice* was
staged twice during Shrovetide – a religious holiday whose mixture of
incongruous qualities parallels those of the play itself – is, I believe,
significant in illuminating many of its themes and patterns for a modern
audience.

A fascinating essay by Rudolph Hassel about the play's religious
conventions has been invaluable in supporting the conceptual approach to
our production, which is set in the eighteenth century during a pre-Lenten
Venetian carnival. Here is Hassel's description of Shrovetide: "It is on the one
hand a time for self-scrutiny, confession, penance, absolution, that time
when, preparatory to the Lenten season, the faithful are shriven. But Shrove
Tuesday was a time of extraordinary license in Renaissance England, called
'carnival,' farewell to the flesh, because it hosts a final outburst of riotous
merry-making just before the penitential restraints of Lent. For centuries it
was the time for confession and shriving, but its chief features were feasting
and boisterous hilarity."

Prescribed biblical passages for Shrovetide reflect this dichotomy between penance and festivity. *The Merchant of Venice* is studded with more biblically derived quotations than any other play by Shakespeare. Most of them come from religious writings that serve as a basis for Shrovetide's period of self-reflection and worship – particularly the Epistles of St. Paul, which John Donne later expanded upon in his Lenten Sermons. One of Donne's messages is that purity, like righteousness, can be vicious as well as virtuous. Our response to Shylock's fate at the end of the trial scene recalls Donne's sermon, which also alludes to the familiar Pauline observation on the breach between Christian precept and practice. As Portia says in her opening scene: "If to do were as easy as to know what were good to do, chapels had been churches, and poor men's cottages princes' palaces. It is a good divine that follows his own instructions; I can easier teach twenty what were good to be done than to be one of the twenty to follow mine own teaching."

The source of Portia's speech is St. Paul's letter to the Romans, which contains passages urging peace between Gentiles and Jews, reminding both of their unity in death and the sacrifice of Christ for all men. Paul's letter also makes a distinction between the old law and the new and between the letter and the spirit of the law, which is a theme examined ironically in the play's trial scene. Portia's speech is a key to one of the play's major themes: God's grace is amazing because of man's universal imperfection. Christians strive for perfection with the full knowledge that they are flawed by original sin and thus can never achieve on their own the state of grace to which the teachings of Christ exhort them. But by understanding their imperfection they can revel in the knowledge that their sins can be forgiven and celebrate their imperfections because they are precisely what make us human. Para-doxically our imperfections assure the perfection of God's perfect grace.

Shylock's puritanically immutable behaviour is a barrier to the Christians' celebration of mutability, and his presence in their midst provides Shakespeare with an all-embracing ironic perspective that forces an audience to reconsider the Christians' standards and actions. Without Shylock's anchor in Judaism, we would be less critical of them, less pressed to examine their faults and virtues. His intractable presence sheds harsh light on their Christianity, which forces us, as it did Renaissance Shrovetide Christians, toward self-examination and reconsideration of our fallibility. Shakespeare chose the popular convention of the "stage Jew" (a character he imbues with nobility and humanity despite Shylock's evil intentions) in order to thrust his other characters into a Shrovetide situation. Shakespeare also parodied the Puritans through Shylock, whose central flaws represent those charac-teristics – intolerance, hypocrisy, self-righteousness – that ultimately caused the Puritans to be forced out of England and into North America. Ironically, however, Shakespeare gives the title character of the play (Antonio, the ostensible "hero" figure) the same characteristics as the "villain."

In *The Merchant of Venice* ideas are introduced like musical themes, and in scene after scene variations and inversions are spun on these ideas. Shakespeare shifts keys as a composer might from, say, major to minor, which subtly alters expectations. Besides noting the similarities between the play's antipodal figures, we are also made aware that the ideas examined in Portia's casket trial are reheard in the trial of Shylock and then re-examined and parodied a third time in the final ring scene. The comic gulling of Old Gobbo by his son Launcelot – a scene shot through with fractured biblical quotations – prophetically parodies the approaching moment when Shylock's daughter, Jessica, steals his wealth and elopes with a Christian. As Shylock's insistence on the "value" of his bond (which he has "consecrated" to God and thus made irrevocable) becomes more adamant, the Christians' pronouncements about the value of mercy and charity come to seem more facile and questionable.

Clearly, *The Merchant of Venice* also elicits disturbing emotional responses from less ecclesiastical audiences than those of the Renaissance. Unfortunately, the play's original meaning has been obscured in the twentieth century by the admixture of horror, guilt, and shame caused by the Holocaust, which has shifted the focus away from the playwright's ironic, comedic examination of the Christian ideals of love's wealth, generosity, mercy, and "bonding" to a much narrower perspective that highlights anti-Semitism. Shakespeare, however, examines all of the play's characters from both positive and negative angles. His stance is compellingly humanistic and ironic. As a result, our trust in the characters' worth is kept in constant jeopardy; we view them not with a jaundiced eye but with astonishment.

The Merchant of Venice will always fascinate, disturb, and satisfy. Our inability to grasp all of its complexities reminds us of our humanity; its partly fairy-tale plot reminds us of those lessons and precepts which we are unable, and often unwilling, to follow or live up to. Ironically, the play reminds us of the life that is as we prepare for the life to come; as we look to a future paradise, we are made aware of the grossness of the flesh and of our need for both judicial structure on earth and God's grace. In *The Merchant of Venice* our morals are questioned, our fallibility celebrated, our ungodliness noted – with wisdom, irony, severity, and compassionate humour.

C Poddubiuk

A Note to
the Reader

The text used in the 1984 Stratford Festival Edition of *The Merchant of Venice* is based upon the Globe Text, with reference to the First Folio. It incorporates generally accepted modern spellings and punctuation. A glossary of Elizabethan and unfamiliar terms appears at the bottom of the pages.

The Act and Scene numbers are given at the top of each right-hand page. The Scene numbers enclosed in brackets in the right-hand margin indicate the way the play was divided for rehearsal purposes at Stratford. During a performance the stage manager would use these Scene numbers to call for light, orchestra, and sound cues.

Also in the right-hand margin is the over-all numerical delineation; the Stratford Festival Edition delineation is enclosed in brackets. The SFE line numbers refer the reader to a set of emendations at the end of the text. These emendations include word changes, line changes, cuts, and additions that were made specifically for the 1984 Stratford Festival Production of *The Merchant of Venice*. Also included are paraphrases of particularly difficult lines.

The 1984 Stratford Festival Production of

The Merchant of Venice

Directed by Mark Lamos
Designed by Christina Poddubiuk
Music by Gary Kulesha
Lighting designed by Michael J. Whitfield

The Cast

VENICE

Antonio, a merchant of Venice		Richard Monette
Salerio		Colm Feore
Solanio	friends to Antonio	Shaun Austin-Olsen
Gratiano		Stephen Russell
Lorenzo,	in love with Jessica	Derek Boyes
Bassanio,	suitor to Portia	Andrew Gillies
Shylock		John Neville
Jessica, his daughter		Seana McKenna
Launcelot Gobbo, his servant		Keith Dinicol
Old Gobbo, Launcelot's father		Mervyn Blake
Tubal, friend to Shylock		Jack Medley
Leonardo, servant to Bassanio		Greg Lawson
Servant to Antonio		Damin Redfern
The Duke of Venice		Lewis Gordon

BELMONT
Portia, a rich heiress — Domini Blythe
Nerissa, her waiting-maid — Heather MacDonald
Stephano ⎫ her servants — David Elliott
Balthasar ⎭ — David Renton
The Prince of Morocco — Jefferson Mappin
The Prince of Arragon — Benedict Campbell
Attendant to Arragon — Tim Whelan
Casket bearers — ⎰ Caro Coltman, Susan Morgan, ⎱ Patrusha Sarakula
Singers — ⎰ Holly Dennison, Janet ⎱ Macdonald, Ron Rees

Masquers, Attendants, Venetians, Elders, Guards: Caro Coltman, Holly Dennison, Daniel Dion, David Elliott, Ernest Harrop, Bill Johnston, Greg Lawson, Toni LoRaso, Ron Rees, David Renton, Patrusha Sarakula, Sally Singal, Brent Stait, Tim Whelan.

Stage Manager: Ihor Sychylo
Assistant Director: Randy Maertz
Assistant Designer: Susan Rome
Assistant Lighting Designer: Elizabeth Asselstine
Assistant Stage Managers: Patricia Henderson and Victoria Klein
Movement Assistant: John Broome

Colm Feore as Salerio, Richard Monette as Antonio,
Shaun Austin-Olsen as Solanio, Andrew Gillies as
Bassanio, Derek Boyes as Lorenzo, Stephen Russell
as Gratiano. Solanio:
    "Here comes Bassanio, your most noble kinsman,
    Gratiano, and Lorenzo. Fare ye well,
    We leave you now with better company."

Act First

Scene 1

[Scene 1]

Venice. A street

Enter Antonio, Salerio, and Solanio

Antonio	In sooth, I know not why I am so sad.	[1]
	It wearies me, you say it wearies you;	
	But how I caught it, found it, or came by it,	
	What stuff 'tis made of, whereof it is born,	
	I am to learn;	
	And such a want-wit sadness makes of me,	
	That I have much ado to know myself.	
Salerio	Your mind is tossing on the ocean,	
	There where your argosies with portly sail,	
	Like signiors and rich burghers on the flood,	10
	Or as it were the pageants of the sea,	
	Do overpeer the petty traffickers,	
	That curtsy to them, do them reverence,	
	As they fly by them with their woven wings.	
Solanio	Believe me, sir, had I such venture forth,	
	The better part of my affections would	
	Be with my hopes abroad. I should be still	
	Plucking the grass to know where sits the wind,	
	Piring in maps for ports, and piers, and roads;	
	And every object that might make me fear	20

---

[1] All numbers in brackets refer to Emendations, pp. 113 – 117.
See also Note, p. 5.
9 **argosies:** large merchant ships
portly: swelling
10 **signiors:** noblemen
11 **pageants:** parade floats, movable platforms
19 **Piring:** peering   **roads:** harbours

	Misfortune to my ventures, out of doubt
	Would make me sad.
Salerio	My wind, cooling my broth,

Salerio My wind, cooling my broth,
Would blow me to an ague, when I thought
What harm a wind too great might do at sea.
I should not see the sandy hour-glass run
But I should think of shallows and of flats,
And see, my wealthy Andrew docks in sand
Vailing her high top lower than her ribs
To kiss her burial. Should I go to church
And see the holy edifice of stone,   30
And not bethink me straight of dangerous rocks,
Which touching but my gentle vessel's side
Would scatter all her spices on the stream,
Enrobe the roaring waters with my silks,
And, in a word, but even now worth this,
And now worth nothing? Shall I have the thought
To think on this, and shall I lack the thought
That such a thing bechanc'd would make me sad?
But tell not me – I know Antonio
Is sad to think upon his merchandise.   40

Antonio Believe me, no; I thank my fortune for it,
My ventures are not in one bottom trusted,
Nor to one place; nor is my whole estate
Upon the fortune of this present year:
Therefore my merchandise makes me not sad.

Solanio Why then, you are in love.

Antonio   Fie, fie!

Solanio Not in love neither? Then let us say you are sad
Because you are not merry; and 'twere as easy
For you to laugh and leap, and say you are merry
Because you are not sad. Now, by two-headed Janus,   [50–56]
Nature hath fram'd strange fellows in her time:
Some that will evermore peep through their eyes,
And laugh like parrots at a bag-piper;
And other of such vinegar aspect,
That they'll not show their teeth in way of smile,
Though Nestor swear the jest be laughable.

Enter Bassanio, Lorenzo, and Gratiano

Here comes Bassanio, your most noble kinsman,
Gratiano, and Lorenzo. Fare ye well,
We leave you now with better company.

27 **Andrew:** the ship's name
28 **Vailing:** lowering **top:** topmast

Salerio	I would have stay'd till I had made you merry,	60
	If worthier friends had not prevented me.	
Antonio	Your worth is very dear in my regard.	
	I take it your own business calls on you,	
	And you embrace the occasion to depart.	
Salerio	Good morrow, my good lords.	
Bassanio	Good signiors both, when shall we laugh? Say, when?	
	You grow exceeding strange: must it be so?	
Salerio	We'll make our leisures to attend on yours.	

Exeunt Salerio and Solanio

Lorenzo	My Lord Bassanio, since you have found Antonio,	
	We two will leave you, but at dinner-time	70
	I pray you have in mind where we must meet.	
Bassanio	I will not fail you.	
Gratiano	You look not well, Signior Antonio,	
	You have too much respect upon the world:	
	They lose it that do buy it with much care,	
	Believe me, you are marvellously chang'd.	
Antonio	I hold the world but as the world, Gratiano,	
	A stage, where every man must play a part,	
	And mine a sad one.	
Gratiano	Let me play the fool,	
	With mirth and laughter let old wrinkles come,	80
	And let my liver rather heat with wine	
	Than my heart cool with mortifying groans.	
	Why should a man whose blood is warm within	
	Sit like his grandsire, cut in alabaster?	
	Sleep when he wakes, and creep into the jaundice	
	By being peevish? I tell thee what, Antonio,	
	I love thee, and it is my love that speaks:	
	There are a sort of men, whose visages	
	Do cream and mantle like a standing pond,	
	And do a wilful stillness entertain,	90
	With purpose to be dress'd in an opinion	
	Of wisdom, gravity, profound conceit,	
	As who should say, "I am Sir Oracle,	
	And when I ope my lips, let no dog bark!"	
	O my Antonio, I do know of these	
	That there only are reputed wise	
	For saying nothing; when I am very sure	
	If they should speak, would almost damn those ears,	
	Which, hearing them, would call their brothers fools.	

---

61 **prevented:** anticipated
74 **respect:** worry
84 **in alabaster:** (on a tomb)
89 **cream and mantle:** have a stagnant covering (like old cream)

11

	I'll tell thee more of this another time.	100
	But fish not with this melancholy bait	[101-02]
	For this fool gudgeon, this opinion.	
	Come, good Lorenzo, fare ye well awhile;	
	I'll end my exhortation after dinner.	
Lorenzo	Well, we will leave you then till dinner-time:	
	I must be one of these same dumb wise men,	
	For Gratiano never lets me speak.	
Gratiano	Well, keep me company but two years moe,	
	Thou shalt not know the sound of thine own tongue.	
Antonio	Fare you well; I'll grow a talker for this gear.	110
Gratiano	Thanks, i' faith, for silence is only commendable	
	In a neat's tongue dried, and a maid not vendible.	

Exeunt Gratiano and Lorenzo

Antonio	Is that anything now?	
Bassanio	Gratiano speaks an infinite deal of nothing more	
	than any man in all Venice. His reasons are as two	
	grains of wheat hid in two bushels of chaff; you	
	shall seek all day ere you find them, and when you	
	have them, they are not worth the search.	
Antonio	Well, tell me now what lady is the same	
	To whom you swore a secret pilgrimage,	120
	That you to-day promis'd to tell me of?	
Bassanio	'Tis not unknown to you, Antonio,	
	How much I have disabled mine estate,	
	By something showing a more swelling port	
	Than my faint means would grant continuance:	
	Nor do I now make moan to be abridg'd	
	From such a noble rate, but my chief care	
	Is to come fairly off from the great debts	
	Wherein my time, something too prodigal,	
	Hath left me gag'd. To you, Antonio,	130
	I owe the most in money and in love,	
	And from your love I have a warranty	
	To unburthen all my plots and purposes	
	How to get clear of all the debts I owe.	
Antonio	I pray you, good Bassanio, let me know it,	
	And if it stand, as you yourself still do,	
	Within the eye of honour, be assur'd,	

108	**moe:** more
110	**gear:** business
112	**neat:** ox **vendible:** marriageable
124	**port:** carriage, demeanour
126	**abridg'd:** cut
127	**rate:** style
130	**gag'd:** pledged

Lorenzo and Bassanio stand by as Antonio speaks:
    "I hold the world but as the world, Gratiano,
    A stage, where every man must play a part,
    And mine a sad one."

	My purse, my person, my extremest means,	
	Lie all unlock'd to your occasions.	
Bassanio	In my school-days, when I had lost one shaft,	140
	I shot his fellow of the self-same flight	
	The self-same way, with more advisèd watch,	
	To find the other forth, and by adventuring both,	
	I oft found both: I urge this childhood proof,	
	Because what follows is pure innocence.	
	I owe you much, and like a wilful youth	
	That which I owe is lost, but if you please	
	To shoot another arrow that self way	
	Which you did shoot the first, I do not doubt,	
	As I will watch the aim, or to find both,	150
	Or bring your latter hazard back again,	
	And thankfully rest debtor for the first.	
Antonio	You know me well, and herein spend but time	
	To wind about my love with circumstance,	
	And out of doubt you do me now more wrong	
	In making question of my uttermost,	
	Than if you had made waste of all I have:	
	Then do but say to me what I should do	
	That in your knowledge may by me be done,	
	And I am prest unto it: therefore speak.	160
Bassanio	In Belmont is a lady richly left,	
	And she is fair, and fairer than that word,	
	Of wondrous virtues; sometimes from her eyes	
	I did receive fair speechless messages:	
	Her name is Portia, nothing undervalued	
	To Cato's daughter, Brutus' Portia,	
	Nor is the wide world ignorant of her worth,	
	For the four winds blow in from every coast	
	Renowned suitors, and her sunny locks	
	Hang on her temples like a golden fleece,	170
	Which makes her seat of Belmont Colchos' strond,	
	And many Jasons come in quest of her.	
	O my Antonio, had I but the means	
	To hold a rival place with one of them,	
	I have a mind presages me such thrift,	
	That I should questionless be fortunate!	

---

139 **occasions:** requirements
140 **shaft:** arrow
141 **his:** its
160 **prest:** ready
166 **Portia:** wife of Brutus (see *Julius Caesar*)
171 **strond:** strand **Colchos:** he owned the
legendary Golden Fleece
172 **Jason** (and the argonauts)

Bassanio to Antonio:
    "In Belmont is a lady richly left,
    And she is fair, and fairer than that word,
    Of wondrous virtues; sometimes from her eyes
    I did receive fair speechless messages:
    Her name is Portia."

Antonio	Thou know'st that all my fortunes are at sea,	
	Neither have I money, nor commodity	
	To raise a present sum; therefore go forth,	
	Try what my credit can in Venice do,	180
	That shall be rack'd even to the uttermost	
	To furnish thee to Belmont to fair Portia.	
	Go, presently inquire, and so will I,	
	Where money is, and I no question make	
	To have it of my trust, or for my sake.	*Exeunt*

Scene 2

Belmont. A room in Portia's house

Enter Portia and Nerissa

Portia	By my troth, Nerissa, my little body is aweary of this great world.	
Nerissa	You would be, sweet madam, if your miseries were in the same abundance as your good fortunes are: and yet, for aught I see, they are as sick that surfeit with too much as they that starve with nothing. It is no mean happiness therefore to be seated in the mean; superfluity comes sooner by white hairs, but competency lives longer.	[8] [9]
Portia	Good sentences, and well pronounc'd.	10
Nerissa	They would be better if well followed.	
Portia	If to do were as easy as to know what were good to do, chapels had been churches, and poor men's cottages princes' palaces. It is a good divine that follows his own instructions; I can easier teach twenty what were good to be done, than to be one of the twenty to follow mine own teaching. The brain may devise laws for the blood, but a hot temper leaps o'er a cold decree, such a hare is madness the youth, to skip o'er the meshes of good	20

181 **rack'd:** strained
8 **mean:** middle
superfluity: superabundance
14 **divine:** preacher

16

counsel the cripple. But this reasoning is not in the fashion to choose me a husband —— O me, the word "choose"! I may neither choose who I would, nor refuse who I dislike, so is the will of a living daughter curb'd by the will of a dead father. Is it not hard, Nerissa, that I cannot choose one, nor refuse none?

Nerissa Your father was ever virtuous, and holy men at their death have good inspirations; therefore the lottery that he hath devised in these three chests of gold, silver, and lead, whereof who chooses his meaning chooses you, will no doubt never be chosen by any rightly, but none who you shall rightly love. But what warmth is there in your affection towards any of these princely suitors that are already come? 30

Portia I pray thee over-name them, and as thou namest them, I will describe them; and according to my description level at my affection.

Nerissa First there is the Neapolitan prince.

Portia Ay, that's a colt indeed, for he doth nothing but talk of his horse, and he makes it a great appropriation to his own good parts that he can shoe him himself. I am much afear'd my lady his mother play'd false with a smith. 40

Nerissa Then there is the County Palatine.

Portia He doth nothing but frown; as who should say, "An you will not have me, choose." He hears merry tales and smiles not; I fear he will prove the weeping philosopher when he grows old, being so full of un-mannerly sadness in his youth. I had rather be married to a death's-head with a bone in his mouth, than either of these. God defend me from these two! 50

Nerissa How say you by the French lord, Monsieur Le Bon?

Portia God made him, and therefore let him pass for a man. In truth I know it is a sin to be a mocker, but he! - why, he hath a horse better than the Neapolitan's, a better bad habit of frowning than the Count Palatine; he is every man in no man; if a throstle sing, he falls straight a capering; he will fence with his own shadow. If I should marry him, I should marry twenty husbands: if he would despise me, I would 60 [61-63]

---

35 **over-name:** name
37 **level at:** assess, determine
41 **County:** Count
46 **An:** If
48 **weeping philosopher:** Heraclitus
50 **death's-head . . . mouth:** skull and crossbones

Portia, played by Domini Blythe, to Nerissa, played
by Heather MacDonald:
"I may neither choose who I would, nor
refuse who I dislike, so is the will of a living
daughter curb'd by the will of a dead father."

	forgive him, for if he love me to madness, I shall	
	never requite him.	
Nerissa	What say you, then, to Falconbridge, the young	
	baron of England?	
Portia	You know I say nothing to him, for he understands	
	not me, nor I him: he hath neither Latin, French,	
	nor Italian, and you will come into the court and	[68–69]
	swear that I have a poor pennyworth in the English.	
	He is a proper man's picture, but alas, who can con-	70
	verse with a dumb-show? How oddly he is suited!	[71–80]
	I think he bought his doublet in Italy, his round	
	hose in France, his bonnet in Germany, and his	
	behaviour everywhere.	
Nerissa	What think you of the Scottish lord, his neighbour?	
Portia	That he hath a neighbourly charity in him, for he	
	borrowed a box of the ear of the Englishman, and	
	swore he would pay him again when he was able: I	
	think the Frenchman became his surety, and seal'd	
	under for another.	80
Nerissa	How like you the young German, the Duke of	
	Saxony's nephew?	
Portia	Very vilely in the morning when he is sober, and	
	most vilely in the afternoon when he is drunk: when	
	he is best, he is a little worse than a man, and when	
	he is worst, he is little better than a beast. An the	
	worst fall that ever fell, I hope I shall make shift to	
	go without him.	
Nerissa	If he should offer to choose, and choose the right	
	casket, you should refuse to perform your father's	90
	will, if you should refuse to accept him.	
Portia	Therefore, for fear of the worst, I pray thee set a deep	
	glass of Rhenish wine on the contrary casket, for if	
	the devil be within, and that temptation without, I	
	know he will choose it. I will do anything, Nerissa,	
	ere I will be married to a sponge.	
Nerissa	You need not fear, lady, the having any of these	
	lords: they have acquainted me with their deter-	
	minations, which is indeed to return to their home,	
	and to trouble you with no more suit, unless you	100
	may be won by some other sort than your father's	
	imposition, depending on the caskets.	
Portia	If I live to be as old as Sibylla, I will die as chaste as	
	Diana, unless I be obtained by the manner of my	

102 **imposition:** will
103 **Sibylla:** the Sibyl
104 **Diana:** goddess of maidenhood (chastity)

John Neville as Shylock:
   "I will buy with you, sell with you, talk with you,
   walk with you, and so following; but I will not eat
   with you, drink with you, nor pray with you."

father's will. I am glad this parcel of wooers are
so reasonable, for there is not one among them but
I dote on his very absence; and I pray God grant
them a fair departure.

Nerissa   Do you not remember, lady, in your father's time, a
Venetian, a scholar and a soldier, that came hither in   110
company of the Marquis of Montferrat?

Portia   Yes, yes, it was Bassanio, as I think so was he call'd.

Nerissa   True, madam, he of all the men that ever my foolish
eyes look'd upon, was the best deserving a fair lady.

Portia   I remember him well, and I remember him worthy
of thy praise.

Enter a Servingman

How, now, what news?

Servingman   The four strangers seek for you, madam, to take   [118]
their leave: and there is a forerunner come from a
fifth, the Prince of Morocco, who brings word the   120
prince his master will be here to-night.

Portia   If I could bid the fifth welcome with so good heart
as I can bid the other four farewell, I should be
glad of his approach. If he have the condition of a
saint, and the complexion of a devil, I had rather he
should shrive me than wive me.
Come, Nerissa. Sirrah, go before.
Whiles we shut the gate upon one wooer, another
knocks at the door.   *Exeunt*

Scene 3

Venice. A public place

Enter Bassanio and Shylock

Shylock   Three thousand ducats, well.
Bassanio   Ay, sir, for three months.
Shylock   For three months, well.
Bassanio   For the which, as I told you, Antonio shall be bound.
Shylock   Antonio shall become bound, well.
Bassanio   May you stead me? Will you pleasure me? Shall I
know your answer?
Shylock   Three thousand ducats for three months, and
Antonio bound.
Bassanio   Your answer to that.   10

6   **stead:** help

Shylock	Antonio is a good man.
Bassanio	Have you heard any imputation to the contrary?
Shylock	Ho, no, no, no, no: my meaning in saying he is a
	good man is to have you understand me that he is
	sufficient, yet his means are in supposition: he hath [15]
	an argosy bound to Tripolis, another to the Indies,
	I understand moreover upon the Rialto, he hath a
	third at Mexico, a fourth for England, and other
	ventures he hath squander'd abroad. But ships are
	but boards, sailors but men, there be land-rats, and 20
	water-rats, water-thieves, and land-thieves – I mean
	pirates – and then there is the peril of waters, winds,
	and rocks: the man is notwithstanding sufficient.
	Three thousand ducats, I think I may take his bond.
Bassanio	Be assur'd you may.
Shylock	I will be assur'd I may; and that I may be assur'd,
	I will bethink me. May I speak with Antonio?
Bassanio	If it please you to dine with us.
Shylock	Yes, to smell pork, to eat of the habitation which
	your prophet the Nazarite conjured the devil into. 30
	I will buy with you, sell with you, talk with you,
	walk with you, and so following; but I will not eat
	with you, drink with you, nor pray with you. What
	news on the Rialto? Who is he comes here?

Enter Antonio

Bassanio	This is Signior Antonio.
Shylock	(*aside*) How like a fawning publican he looks!
	I hate him for he is a Christian;
	But more, for that in low simplicity
	He lends out money gratis, and brings down
	The rate of usance here with us in Venice. 40
	If I can catch him once upon the hip,
	I will feed fat the ancient grudge I bear him.
	He hates our sacred nation, and he rails,
	Even there where merchants most do congregate,
	On me, my bargains, and my well-won thrift,
	Which he calls interest. Cursèd be my tribe
	If I forgive him!
Bassanio	Shylock, do you hear?
Shylock	I am debating of my present store,
	And by the near guess of my memory
	I cannot instantly raise up the gross 50

---

36 **publican:** Roman tax collector
40 **usance:** usury
41 **upon the hip:** at a disadvantage (wrestling term)

	Of full three thousand ducats: what of that?
	Tubal, a wealthy Hebrew of my tribe,
	Will furnish me. But soft! How many months
	Do you desire? (*To Antonio*) Rest you fair, good
	signior,
	Your worship was the last man in our mouths.
Antonio	Shylock, albeit I neither lend nor borrow
	By taking nor by giving in excess,
	Yet, to supply the ripe wants of my friend,
	I'll break a custom. Is he yet possess'd
	How much ye would?
Shylock	Ay, ay, three thousand ducats.
Antonio	And for three months.
Shylock	I had forgot, three months, you told me so.
	Well then, your bond; and let me see, but hear
	you,
	Methoughts you said you neither lend nor borrow
	Upon advantage.
Antonio	I do never use it.
Shylock	When Jacob graz'd his uncle Laban's sheet –
	This Jacob from our holy Abram was,
	As his wise mother wrought in his behalf,
	The third possessor; ay, he was the third –
Antonio	And what of him? Did he take interest?
Shylock	No, not take interest, not, as you would say,
	Directly interest: mark what Jacob did.
	When Laban and himself were compromis'd
	That all the eanlings which were streak'd and pied
	Should fall as Jacob's hire, the ewes being rank
	In end of autumn turnèd to the rams,
	And when the work of generation was
	Between these woolly breeders in the act,
	The skilful shepherd pill'd me certain wands,
	And in the doing of the deed of kind
	He stuck them up before the fulsome ewes,
	Who, then conceiving, did in eaning time
	Fall parti-colour'd lambs, and those were Jacob's.
	This was a way to thrive, and he was blest:
	And thrift is blessing if men steal it not.
Antonio	This was a venture, sir, that Jacob serv'd for;
	A thing not in his power to bring to pass,
	But sway'd and fashion'd by the hand of heaven.

Line numbers: 60, [66–85], 70, [73], 80

57 **excess:** interest
59 **possess'd:** informed
74 **eanlings:** lambs
75 **rank:** in heat
79 **pill'd:** peeled bark from
83 **Fall:** give birth to

	Was this inserted to make interest good?	
	Or is your gold and silver ewes and rams?	90
Shylock	I cannot tell; I make it breed as fast.	
	But note me, signior –	
Antonio	Mark you this, Bassanio,	

Antonio   Mark you this, Bassanio,
The devil can cite Scripture for his purpose;
An evil soul producing holy witness
Is like a villain with a smiling cheek,
A goodly apple rotten at the heart.
O, what a goodly outside falsehood hath!

Shylock   Three thousand ducats, 'tis a good round sum.
Three months from twelve; then, let me see, the
     rate –

Antonio   Well, Shylock, shall we be beholding to you?   100
Shylock   Signior Antonio, many a time and oft
In the Rialto you have rated me
About my moneys and my usances:
Still have I borne it with a patient shrug,
For sufferance is the badge of all our tribe.
You call me misbeliever, cut-throat dog,
And spit upon my Jewish gaberdine,
And all for use of that which is mine own.
Well then, it now appears you need my help:
Go to then, you come to me, and you say,   110
"Shylock, we would have moneys": you say so!
You that did void your rheum upon my beard,
And foot me as you spurn a stranger cur
Over your threshold, moneys is your suit.
What should I say to you? Should I not say,
"Hath a dog money? Is it possible
A cur can lend three thousand ducats?" Or
Shall I bend low, and in a bondman's key,
With bated breath, and whispering humbleness,
Say this –   120
"Fair sir, you spit on me on Wednesday last;
You spurn'd me such a day; another time
You call'd me dog; and for these courtesies
I'll lend you thus much moneys"?

Antonio   I am as like to call thee so again,
To spit on thee again, to spurn thee too.
If thou wilt lend this money, lend it not
As to thy friends, for when did friendship take

89	**inserted:** mentioned	112	**rheum:** spittle
102	**rated:** berated	113	**foot:** kick
105	**sufferance:** endurance		

Shylock
John Neville
The Merchant
Of Venice
Stratford 1954

C. Poddubiuk

	A breed for barren metal of his friend?	
	But lend it rather to thine enemy,	130
	Who if he break, thou may'st with better face	
	Exact the penalty.	
Shylock	Why, look you how you storm!	
	I would be friends with you, and have your love,	
	Forget the shames that you have stain'd me with,	
	Supply your present wants, and take no doit	
	Of usance for my moneys, and you'll not hear me:	
	This is kind I offer.	
Bassanio	This were kindness.	
Shylock	This kindness will I show;	
	Go with me to a notary, seal me there	
	Your single bond, and, in a merry sport,	140
	If you repay me not on such a day,	
	In such a place, such sum or sums as are	
	Express'd in the condition, let the forfeit	
	Be nominated for an equal pound	
	Of your fair flesh, to be cut off and taken	
	In what part of your body pleaseth me.	
Antonio	Content, i' faith, I'll seal to such a bond,	
	And say there is much kindness in the Jew.	
Bassanio	You shall not seal to such a bond for me,	
	I'll rather dwell in my necessity.	150
Antonio	Why, fear not, man, I will not forfeit it;	
	Within these two months, that's a month before	
	This bond expires, I do expect return	
	Of thrice three times the value of this bond.	
Shylock	O father Abram, what these Christians are,	
	Whose own hard dealings teaches them suspect	
	The thoughts of others! Pray you, tell me this:	
	If he should break his day, what should I gain	
	By the exaction of the forfeiture?	
	A pound of man's flesh taken from a man	160
	Is not so estimable, profitable neither,	
	As flesh of muttons, beefs, or goats. I say,	
	To buy his favour, I extend this friendship;	
	If he will take it, so, if not, adieu,	
	And, for my love, I pray you wrong me not.	
Antonio	Yes, Shylock, I will seal unto this bond.	
Shylock	Then meet me forthwith at the notary's;	
	Give him direction for this merry bond,	

---

129 **A breed for:** a breeding of
of: from

135 **doit:** small amount
165 **love:** kindness

And I will go and purse the ducats straight,
See to my house, left in the fearful guard   170
Of an unthrifty knave; and presently
I'll be with you.

Antonio   Hie thee, gentle Jew.   *Exit Shylock*
The Hebrew will turn Christian: he grows kind.

Bassanio   I like not fair terms, and a villain's mind.

Antonio   Come on, in this there can be no dismay,
My ships come home a month before the day.

                                                  Exeunt

170   **fearful:** untrustworthy

Act Second

Scene 1

[Scene 4]

Belmont. A room in Portia's house

Enter the Prince of Morocco and three or four followers
with Portia, Nerissa, and their train

Morocco	Mislike me not for my complexion,
	The shadowed livery of the burnish'd sun,
	To whom I am a neighbour, and near bred.
	Bring me the fairest creature northward born,
	Where Phoebus' fire scarce thaws the icicles,
	And let us make incision for your love,
	To prove whose blood is reddest, his or mine.
	I tell thee, lady, this aspect of mine
	Hath fear'd the valiant: by my love, I swear
	The best-regarded virgins of our clime
	Hath lov'd it too. I would not change this hue,
	Except to steal your thoughts, my gentle queen.
Portia	In terms of choice I am not solely led
	By nice direction of a maiden's eyes;
	Besides, the lottery of my destiny
	Bars me the right of voluntary choosing:
	But if my father had not scanted me,
	And hedg'd me by his wit to yield myself
	His wife who wins me by that means I told you,
	Yourself, renownèd prince, then stood as fair
	As any comer I have look'd on yet
	For my affection.

10

20

---

9 **fear'd:** put fear in
14 **nice:** particular
17 **scanted:** restricted

Portia:
  "In terms of choice I am not solely led
  By nice directions of a maiden's eyes;
  Besides, the lottery of my destiny
  Bars me the right of voluntary choosing."

Morocco	Even for that I thank you.
	Therefore I pray you lead me to the caskets
	To try my fortune. By this scimitar
	That slew the Sophy, and a Persian prince
	That won three fields of Sultan Solyman,
	I would outstare the sternest eyes that look,
	Outbrave the heart most daring on the earth,
	Pluck the young sucking cubs from the she-bear,
	Yea, mock the lion when he roars for prey,
	To win thee, lady. But, alas the while,
	If Hercules and Lichas play at dice
	Which is the better man, the greater throw
	May turn by fortune from the weaker hand:
	So is Alcides beaten by his page,
	And so may I, blind fortune leading me,
	Miss that which one unworthier may attain,
	And die with grieving.
Portia	You must take your chance,
	And either not attempt to choose at all,
	Or swear before you choose, if you choose wrong,
	Never to speak to lady afterward
	In way of marriage; therefore be advis'd.
Morocco	Nor will not; come, bring me unto my chance.
Portia	First forward to the temple; after dinner
	Your hazard shall be made.
Morocco	Good fortune then,
	To make me blest or cursed'st among men!

30
[31–38]

40

Cornets, and exeunt

Scene 2

Venice. A street

Enter Launcelot

Launcelot	Certainly, my conscience will serve me to run from
	this Jew my master: the fiend is at mine elbow,
	and tempts me, saying to me, "Gobbo, Launcelot
	Gobbo, good Launcelot," or "good Gobbo," or

25 **Sophy:** Shah of Persia
26 **fields:** battles

"good Launcelot Gobbo, use your legs, take the
start, run away." My conscience says, "No; take
heed, honest Launcelot, take heed, honest Gobbo,"
or, as aforesaid, "honest Launcelot Gobbo, do not
run, scorn running with thy heels." Well, the
most courageous fiend bids me pack, "*Via!*" says   10
the fiend, "away!" says the fiend, "for the heavens,
rouse up a brave mind," says the fiend, "and run."
Well, my conscience, hanging about the neck of my
heart, says very wisely to me, "My honest friend
Launcelot, being an honest man's son," – or rather
an honest woman's son; – for, indeed, my father did
something smack, something grow to – he had a
kind of taste; – well, my conscience says, "Launcelot,
budge not," "budge," says the fiend, "budge not,"
says my conscience, "conscience," say I, "you counsel   20
well," "fiend," say I, "you counsel well:" to be rul'd
by my conscience, I should stay with the Jew my
master, who, God bless the mark, is a kind of
devil; and, to run away from the Jew, I should be
ruled by the fiend, who, saving your reverence, is the
devil himself. Certainly the Jew is the very devil
incarnation, and, in my conscience, my conscience is
but a kind of hard conscience, to offer to counsel me
to stay with the Jew; the fiend gives the more
friendly counsel: I will run, fiend, my heels are at   30
your commandment, I will run.

Enter Old Gobbo, with a basket

Gobbo   Master young-man, you, I pray you, which is the
way to master Jew's?

Launcelot   (*aside*) O heavens, this is my true-begotten father,
who, being more than sand-blind, high-gravel blind,
knows me not; I will try confusions with him.

Gobbo   Master young gentleman, I pray you which is the
way to master Jew's?

Launcelot   Turn up on your right hand at the next turning, but
at the next turning of all on your left; marry, at the   40
very next turning, turn of no hand, but turn down
indirectly to the Jew's house.

Gobbo   Be God's sonties, 'twill be a hard way to hit; can

---

10 **Via:** Away; be off
17 **something smack:** something of a bad smell
    grow to: have a bad taste
35 **sand-blind:** half-blind
    high-gravel blind: almost wholly blind
43 **Sonties:** saints

Launcelot, played by Keith Dinicol, and Old
Gobbo, played by Mervyn Blake.
Launcelot: "Do I look like a cudgel or a hovel-post,
    a staff or a prop? Do you know me, father?"

	you tell me whether one Launcelot, that dwells with him, dwell with him or no?
Launcelot	Talk of young Master Launcelot? (*Aside*) Mark me now, now will I raise the waters – talk you of young Master Launcelot?
Gobbo	No master, sir, but a poor man's son; his father, though I say 't, is an honest exceeding poor man, and, God be thanked, well to live.
Launcelot	Well, let his father be what a' will, we talk of young Master Launcelot.
Gobbo	Your worship's friend, and Launcelot, sir.
Launcelot	But I pray you, ergo, old man, ergo, I beseech you, talk you of young Master Launcelot?
Gobbo	Of Launcelot, an 't please your mastership.
Launcelot	Ergo, Master Launcelot; talk not of Master Launcelot, father, for the young gentleman, according to Fates and Destinies, and such odd sayings, the Sisters Three, and such branches of learning, is indeed deceased; or, as you would say in plain terms, gone to heaven.
Gobbo	Marry, God forbid! The boy was the very staff of my age, my very prop.
Launcelot	Do I look like a cudgel or a hovel-post, a staff, or a prop? Do you know me, father?
Gobbo	Alack the day, I know you not, young gentleman, but, I pray you tell me, is my boy, God rest his soul, alive or dead?
Launcelot	Do you not know me, father?
Gobbo	Alack, air, I am sand-blind, I know you not.
Launcelot	Nay, indeed, if you had your eyes you might fail of the knowing me: it is a wise father that knows his own child. Well, old man, I will tell you news of your son. Give me your blessing, truth will come to light, murder cannot be hid long, a man's son may, but in the end truth will out.
Gobbo	Pray you, sir, stand up, I am sure you are not Launcelot, my boy.
Launcelot	Pray you, let's have no more fooling about it, but give me your blessing: I am Launcelot, your boy that was, your son that is, your child that shall be.
Gobbo	I cannot think you are my son.
Launcelot	I know not what I shall think of that: but I am

Line numbers in margin: 50, 60, 70, 80

---

51 **well to live:** well-to-do
60 **Sisters Three:** the Fates
66 **hovel-post:** post that props up an old house

	Launcelot, the Jew's man, and I am sure Margery
	your wife is my mother.
Gobbo	Her name is Margery, indeed; I'll be sworn, if thou
	be Launcelot, thou are mine own flesh and blood.
	Lord worshipp'd might he be, what a beard hast thou
	got! Thou hast got more hair on thy chin than
	Dobbin my fill-horse has on his tail.

Gobbo Her name is Margery, indeed; I'll be sworn, if thou
be Launcelot, thou are mine own flesh and blood.
Lord worshipp'd might he be, what a beard hast thou   90
got! Thou hast got more hair on thy chin than
Dobbin my fill-horse has on his tail.

Launcelot It should seem, then, that Dobbin's tail grows back-
ward: I am sure he had more hair of his tail than I
have of my face when I last saw him.

Gobbo Lord, how art thou chang'd! How dost thou and
thy master agree? I have brought him a present.
How 'gree you now?

Launcelot Well, well: but for mine own part, as I have set
up my rest to run away, so I will not rest till I   100
have run some ground. My master's a very Jew:
give him a present? Give him a halter: I am
famish'd in his service; you may tell every finger
I have with my ribs. Father, I am glad you are
come; give me your present to one Master Bassanio,
who indeed gives rare new liveries; if I serve not
him, I will run as far as God has any ground. O
rare fortune! Here comes the man; to him, father,
for I am a Jew if I serve the Jew any longer.

Enter Bassanio with Leonardo and followers

Bassanio You may do so, but let it be so hasted that supper   110
be ready at the farthest by five of the clock: see
these letters delivered, put the liveries to making,
and desire Gratiano to come anon to my lodging.

Exit a servant

Launcelot To him, father.

Gobbo God bless your worship!

Bassanio Gramercy! Wouldst thou aught with me?

Gobbo Here's my son, sir, a poor boy –

Launcelot Not a poor boy, but the rich Jew's man, that
would, sir, as my father shall specify –

Gobbo He hath a great infection, sir, as one would say, to   120
serve –

Launcelot Indeed, the short and the long is, I serve the Jew,
and have a desire, as my father shall specify, –

Gobbo His master and he, saving your worship's reverence,
are scarce cater-cousins, –

---

92 **fill-horse:** cart horse
99 **set up my rest:** made up my mind
106 **liveries:** uniforms
120 **infection:** desire (malapropism)
125 **cater-cousins:** intimates

Launcelot	To be brief, the very truth is, that the Jew having done me wrong, doth cause me, as my father being I hope an old man shall frutify unto you, –
Gobbo	I have here a dish of doves that I would bestow upon your worship, and my suit is, – 130
Launcelot	In very brief, the suit is impertinent to myself, as your worship shall know by this honest old man, and, though I say it, though old man, yet poor man, my father.
Bassanio	One speak for both. What would you?
Launcelot	Serve you, sir.
Gobbo	That is the very defect of the matter, sir.
Bassanio	I know thee well, thou hast obtain'd thy suit; Shylock thy master spoke with me this day, And hath preferr'd thee, if it be preferment 140 To leave a rich Jew's service, to become The follower of so poor a gentleman.
Launcelot	The old proverb is very well parted between my master Shylock and you, sir; you have the grace of God, sir, and he hath enough.
Bassanio	Thou speak'st it well; go, father, with thy son. Take leave of thy old master, and inquire My lodging out; give him a livery More guarded than his fellows': see it done.
Launcelot	Father, in. I cannot get a service, no, I have ne'er [150–59] a tongue in my head. Well, if any man in Italy have a fairer table which doth offer to swear upon a book, I shall have good fortune. Go to, here's a simple line of life, here's a small trifle of wives; alas, fifteen wives is nothing, eleven widows and nine maids is a simple coming-in for one man, and then to 'scape drowning thrice, and to be in peril of my life with the edge of a feather-bed, here are simple scapes. Well, if Fortune be a woman, she's a good wench for this gear. Father, come, I'll take my leave of [160] the Jew in the twinkling.

Exeunt Launcelot and Old Gobbo

Bassanio	I pray thee, good Leonardo, think on this: These things being bought and orderly bestow'd, Return in haste, for I do feast to-night My best-esteem'd acquaintance: hie thee, go.
Leonardo	My best endeavours shall be done herein.

143 **The old proverb:** "God's gear is grace enough"
149 **guarded:** elaborate

Enter Gratiano

Gratiano Where's your master?

Leonardo Yonder, sir, he walks.

Exit

Gratiano Signior Bassanio, –

Bassanio Gratiano!

Gratiano I have suit to you.

Bassanio You have obtain'd it. 170

Gratiano You must not deny me; I must go with you to
Belmont.

Bassanio Why then, you must. But hear thee, Gratiano:
Thou art too wild, too rude, and bold of voice,
Parts that become thee happily enough
And in such eyes as ours appear not faults,
But where thou art not known, why there they show
Something too liberal: pray thee, take pain
To allay with some cold drops of modesty
Thy skipping spirit, lest through thy wild behaviour 180
I be misconster'd in the place I go to,
And lose my hopes.

Gratiano Signior Bassanio, hear me:
If I do not put on a sober habit,
Talk with respect, and swear but now and then,
Wear prayer-books in my pocket, look demurely,
Nay more, while grace is saying, hood mine eyes
Thus with my hat, and sign, and say "amen,"
Use all the observance of civility,
Like one well studied in a sad ostent
To please his grandam, never trust me more. 190

Bassanio Well, we shall see your bearing.

Gratiano Nay, but I bar to-night, you shall not gauge me
By what we do to-night.

Bassanio No, that were pity:
I would entreat you rather to put on
Your boldest suit of mirth, for we have friends
That purpose merriment. But fare you well,
I have some business.

Gratiano And I must to Lorenzo and the rest,
But we will visit you at supper-time. *Exeunt*

---

181 **misconster'd:** misinterpreted
189 **sad ostent:** sober bearing

Scene 3

[Scene 6]

The same. A room in Shylock's house

Enter Jessica and Launcelot

Jessica	I am sorry thou wilt leave my father so;
	Our house is hell, and thou, a merry devil,
	Didst rob it of some taste of tediousness.
	But fare thee well, there is a ducat for thee,
	And, Launcelot, soon at supper shalt thou see
	Lorenzo, who is thy new master's guest;
	Give him this letter; do it secretly;
	And so farewell: I would not have my father
	See me in talk with thee.
Launcelot	Adieu! Tears exhibit my tongue. Most beautiful 10
	pagan, most sweet Jew! If a Christian do not play
	the knave, and get thee, I am much deceived. But
	adieu; these foolish drops do something drown my
	manly spirit: adieu.
Jessica	Farewell, good Launcelot. *Exit Launcelot*
	Alack, what heinous sin is it in me
	To be asham'd to be my father's child!
	But though I am a daughter to his blood,
	I am not to his manners. O Lorenzo,
	If thou keep promise I shall end this strife, 20
	Become a Christian and thy loving wife. *Exit*

Scene 4

[Scene 7]

The same. A street

Enter Gratiano, Lorenzo, Salerio, and Solanio

Lorenzo	Nay, we will slink away in supper-time,
	Disguise us at my lodging, and return
	All in an hour.
Gratiano	We have not made good preparation.
Salerio	We have not spoke us yet of torch-bearers.
Solanio	'Tis vile, unless it may be quaintly order'd,
	And better in my mind not undertook.

---

19   **manners:** character
6   **quaintly:** deftly

Lorenzo	'Tis now but four o'clock; we have two hours
	To furnish us.

Enter Launcelot, with a letter

	Friend Launcelot, what's the news?
Launcelot	An it shall please you to break up this, it shall seem 10
	to signify.
Lorenzo	I know the hand, in faith, 'tis a fair hand,
	And whiter than the paper it writ on
	Is the fair hand that writ.
Gratiano	Love-news, in faith.
Launcelot	By your leave, sir.
Lorenzo	Whither goest thou?
Launcelot	Marry, sir, to bid my old master the Jew to sup
	tonight with my new master the Christian.
Lorenzo	Hold, here, take this; tell gentle Jessica
	I will not fail her; speak it privately. 20
	Go, gentlemen, *Exit Launcelot*
	Will you prepare you for this masque to-night?
	I am provided of a torch-bearer.
Salerio	Ay, marry, I'll be gone about it straight.
Solanio	And so will I.
Lorenzo	Meet me and Gratiano
	At Gratiano's lodging some hour hence.
Salerio	'Tis good we do so. *Exeunt Salerio and Solanio*
Gratiano	Was not that letter from fair Jessica?
Lorenzo	I must needs tell thee all. She hath directed
	How I shall take her from her father's house, 30
	What gold and jewels she is furnish'd with,
	What page's suit she hath in readiness.
	If e'er the Jew her father come to heaven,
	It will be for his gentle daughter's sake,
	And never dare misfortune cross her foot,
	Unless she do it under this excuse,
	That she is issue to a faithless Jew.
	Come, go with me, peruse this as thou goest:
	Fair Jessica shall be my torch-bearer. *Exeunt*

35 **foot**: path

Scene 5

[Scene 8]

The same. Before Shylock's house

Enter Shylock and Launcelot

Shylock	Well, thou shalt see, thy eyes shall be thy judge,
	The difference of old Shylock and Bassanio: –
	What, Jessica! – thou shalt not gormandise,
	As thou hast done with me: – What, Jessica! –
	And sleep, and snore, and rend apparel out; –
	Why, Jessica, I say!
Launcelot	Why, Jessica!
Shylock	Who bids thee call? I do not bid thee call.
Launcelot	Your worship was wont to tell me I could do
	nothing without bidding.

Enter Jessica

Jessica	Call you? What is your will?	10
Shylock	I am bid forth to supper, Jessica;	
	There are my keys. But wherefore should I go?	
	I am not bid for love; they flatter me:	
	But yet I'll go in hate, to feed upon	
	The prodigal Christian. Jessica, my girl,	
	Look to my house; I am right loath to go;	
	There is some ill a-brewing towards my rest,	
	For I did dream of money-bags to-night.	
Launcelot	I beseech you, sir, go; my young master doth expect	
	your reproach.	20
Shylock	So do I his.	
Launcelot	And they have conspired together; I will not say	
	you shall see a masque, but if you do, then it was	[23–27]
	not for nothing that my nose fell a-bleeding on Black-	
	Monday last, at six o'clock i' the morning, falling	
	out that year on Ash-Wednesday was four year, in	
	the afternoon.	
Shylock	What, are there masques? Hear you me, Jessica:	
	Lock up my doors, and when your hear the drum	
	And the vile squealing of the wry-neck'd fife,	30
	Clamber not you up to the casements then,	
	Nor thrust your head into the public street	
	To gaze on Christian fools with varnish'd faces;	
	But stop my house's ears, I mean my casements,	

---

20   **reproach:** approach (malapropism)
33   **varnish'd:** made up, masked

	Let not the sound of shallow foppery enter	
	My sober house. By Jacob's staff I swear	
	I have no mind of feasting forth to-night:	
	But I will go. Go you before me, sirrah,	
	Say I will come.	

Launcelot I will go before, sir. Mistress, look out at window   40
for all this:
    "There will come a Christian by,
      Will be worth a Jewess' eye."   *Exit*

Shylock What says that fool of Hagar's offspring, ha?

Jessica His words were, "Farewell, mistress," nothing else.

Shylock The patch is kind enough, but a huge feeder;
Snail-slow in profit, and he sleeps by day
More than the wild-cat: drones hive not with me,
Therefore I part with him, and part with him
To one that I would have him help to waste   50
His borrow'd purse. Well, Jessica, go in:
Perhaps I will return immediately.
Do as I bid you, shut doors after you:
Fast bind, fast find,
A proverb never stale in thrifty mind.   *Exit*

Jessica Farewell, and if my fortune be not crost,
I have a father, you a daughter, lost.   *Exit*

Scene 6

[Scene 9]

Enter Gratiano and Salerio, masked

Gratiano This is the pent-house under which Lorenzo
Desir'd us to make stand.

Salerio   His hour is almost past.

Gratiano And it is marvel he out-dwells his hour;
For lovers ever run before the clock.

Salerio O, ten times faster Venus' pigeons fly
To seal love's bonds new-made, than they are wont
To keep obligèd faith unforfeited!

Gratiano That ever holds: who riseth from a feast
With that keen appetite that he sits down?

---

35 **shallow foppery:** silly revelry
44 **Hagar:** a Gentile bondwoman, mother of Ishmael
46 **patch:** fool
1 **pent-house:** porch
5 **Venus' pigeons:** doves that drew her chariot

Shylock to Jessica, played by Seana McKenna:
    "... Jessica, my girl,
    Look to my house; I am right loath to go;
    There is some ill a-brewing towards my rest ..."

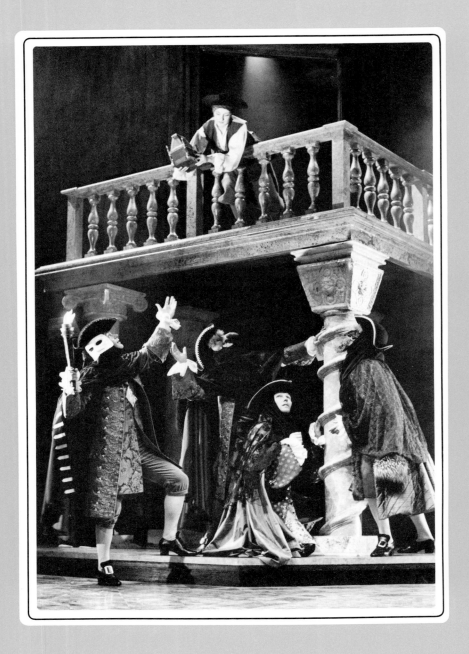

Jessica to Lorenzo as Salerio, Gratiano, and
Solanio look on:
> "Here, catch this casket; it is worth the pains.
> I am glad 'tis night, you do not look on me,
> For I am much asham'd of my exchange."

	Where is the horse that doth untread again	10
	His tedious measures with the unbated fire	
	That he did pace them first? All things that are	
	Are with more spirit chasèd than enjoy'd.	
	How like a younger or a prodigal	
	The scarfèd bark puts from her native bay,	
	Hugg'd and embracèd by the strumpet wind;	
	How like the prodigal doth she return,	
	With over-weather'd ribs and ragged sails,	
	Lean, rent, and beggar'd by the strumpet wind!	

Salerio   Here comes Lorenzo; more of this hereafter.   20

Enter Lorenzo

Lorenzo   Sweet friends, your patience for my long abode;
Not I, but my affairs, have made you wait:
When you shall please to play the thieves for wives,
I'll watch as long for you then. Approach;
Here dwells my father Jew. Ho! Who's within?

Enter Jessica, above, in boy's clothes

Jessica   Who are you? Tell me, for more certainty,
Albeit I'll swear that I do know your tongue.

Lorenzo   Lorenzo, and thy love.

Jessica   Lorenzo certain, and my love indeed,
For who love I so much? And now who knows   30
But you, Lorenzo, whether I am yours?

Lorenzo   Heaven and thy thoughts are witness that thou art.

Jessica   Here, catch this casket; it is worth the pains.
I am glad 'tis night, you do not look on me,
For I am much asham'd of my exchange:
But love is blind, and lovers cannot see
The pretty follies that themselves commit,
For it they could, Cupid himself would blush
To see me thus transformèd to a boy.

Lorenzo   Descend, for you must be my torch-bearer.   40

Jessica   What, must I hold a candle to my shames?
They in themselves, good sooth, are too too light.
Why, 'tis an office of discovery, love,
And I should be obscur'd.

Lorenzo   So are you, sweet,
Even in the lovely garnish of a boy.
But come at once,

---

11   **unbated:** unabated
15   **scarfèd bark:** decorated ship
19   **strumpet:** like harlots of the Prodigal parable (St. Luke 15)
21   **abode:** delay
35   **exchange:** disguise (as a boy)

Venetian Ladies
The Merchant of
Venice
C. Poddubiuk

	For the close night doth play the runaway,	
	And we are stay'd for at Bassanio's feast.	
Jessica	I will make fast the doors and gild myself	
	With some moe ducats, and be with you straight.	50

Exit above

Gratiano	Now, by my hood, a gentle, and no Jew.
Lorenzo	Beshrew me but I love her heartily,
	For she is wise, if I can judge of her,
	And fair she is, if that mine eyes be true,
	And true she is, as she hath prov'd herself;
	And therefore like herself, wise, fair, and true,
	Shall she be placed in my constant soul.

Enter Jessica, below

| | What, art thou come? On, gentlemen, away! |
| | Our masquing mates by this time for us stay. |

Exit with Jessica and Salerio

Enter Antonio

Antonio	Who's there?	60
Gratiano	Signior Antonio?	
Antonio	Fie, fie, Gratiano, where are all the rest?	
	'Tis nine o'clock, our friends all stay for you:	
	No masque to-night, the wind is come about,	
	Bassanio presently will go aboard:	
	I have sent twenty out to seek for you.	
Gratiano	I am glad on 't; I desire no more delight	
	Than to be under sail, and gone to-night.	*Exeunt*

Scene 7

[Scene 10]

Belmont. A room in Portia's house

Enter Portia, with the Prince of Morocco, and her trains

Portia	Go, draw aside the curtains, and discover	[1]
	The several caskets to this noble prince.	
	Now make your choice.	
Morocco	This first of gold, who this inscription bears,	
	"Who chooseth me, shall gain what many men desire;"	
	The second silver, which this promise carries,	
	"Who chooseth me, shall get as much as he deserves;"	
	This third, dull lead, with warning all as blunt,	

---

51 **gentle:** gentlewoman, with obvious play on "gentile."

"Who chooseth me, must give and hazard all he hath."
How shall I know if I do choose the right?   10

Portia   The one of them contains my picture, prince;
If you choose that, then I am yours withal.

Morocco   Some god direct my judgement! Let me see;
I will survey the inscriptions, back again;
What says this leaden casket?
"Who chooseth me, must give and hazard all he hath."
Must give – for what? For lead, hazard for lead?
This casket threatens; men that hazard all
Do it in hope of fair advantages:
A golden mind stoops not to shows of dross.   20
I'll then nor give nor hazard aught for lead.
What says the silver with her virgin hue?
"Who chooseth me, shall get as much as he deserves."
As much as he deserves? Pause there, Morocco,
And weigh thy value with an even hand:
If thou be'st rated by thy estimation,
Thou dost deserve enough, and yet enough
May not extend so far as to the lady:
And yet to be afeard of my deserving
Were but a weak disabling of myself.   30
As much as I deserve? Why, that's the lady:
I do in birth deserve her, and in fortunes,
In graces, and in qualities of breeding;
But more than these, in love I do deserve.
What if I stray'd no further, but chose here?
Let's see once more this saying grav'd in gold:
"Who chooseth me, shall gain what many men desire."
Why, that's the lady; all the world desires her;
From the four corners of the earth they come
To kiss this shrine, this mortal breathing saint: 40
The Hyrcanian deserts, and the vasty wilds   [41–47]
Of wide Arabia are as throughfares now
For princes to come view fair Portia:
The watery kingdom, whose ambitious head
Spits in the face of heaven, is no bar
To stop the foreign spirits, but they come
As o'er a brook to see fair Portia.
One of these three contains her heavenly picture;
Is 't like that lead contains her? 'Twere damnation
To think so base a thought, it were too gross   50
To rib her cerecloth in the obscure grave;

---

21   **dross:** worthless metal
51   **rib:** enclose   **cerecloth:** enbalming sheet

Jefferson Mappin as the Prince of Morocco:
   "O hell! What have we here?
   A carrion Death, within whose empty eye
   There is a written scroll! I'll read the writing."

Or shall I think in silver she's immur'd,
Being ten times undervalued to tried gold?
O sinful thought! Never so rich a gem
Was set in worse than gold. They have in England
A coin that bears the figure of an angel
Stamped in gold, but that's insculp'd upon;
But there an angel in a golden bed
Lies all within. Deliver me the key:
Here do I choose, and thrive I as I may!   60

Portia There, take it, prince, and if my form lie there,
Then I am yours!   *He unlocks the golden casket*

Morocco   O hell! What have we here?
A carrion Death, within whose empty eye
There is a written scroll! I'll read the writing.

(*Reads*) "All that glisters is not gold,
Often have you heard that told,
Many a man his life hath sold
But my outside to behold,
Gilded tombs do worms infold:
Had you been as wise as bold,   70
Young in limbs, in judgement old,
Your answer had not been inscroll'd,
Fare you well, your suit is cold."

Cold indeed, and labour lost,
Then farewell heat, and welcome frost!
Portia, adieu, I have too griev'd a heart
To take a tedious leave: thus losers part.
    Exit with his train. Flourish of cornets

Portia A gentle riddance. Draw the curtains, go.   [78]
Let all of his complexion choose me so. *Exeunt*

Scene 8   [Scene 11]

Venice. A street

Enter Salerio and Solanio

Salerio Why, man, I saw Bassanio under sail,
With him is Gratiano gone along;
And in their ship I am sure Lorenzo is not.
Solanio The villain Jew with outcries rais'd the Duke,
Who went with him to search Bassanio's ship.

79 **complexion:** character; appearance

Solanio to Salerio:
"I never heard a passion so confus'd,
So strange, outrageous, and so variable,
As the dog Jew did utter in the streets,
'My daughter! O my ducats! O my daughter!
Fled with a Christian! O my Christian ducats!'"

Salerio	He came too late, the ship was under sail,
	But there the Duke was given to understand
	That in a gondola were seen together
	Lorenzo and his amorous Jessica:
	Besides, Antonio certified the Duke 10
	They were not with Bassanio in his ship.
Solanio	I never heard a passion so confus'd,
	So strange, outrageous, and so variable,
	As the dog Jew did utter in the streets,
	"My daughter! O my ducats! O my daughter!
	Fled with a Christian! O my Christian ducats!
	Justice! The law! My ducats, and my daughter,
	A sealèd bag, two sealèd bags of ducats,
	Of double ducats, stolen from me by my daughter!
	And jewels, two stones, two rich and precious stones, 20
	Stolen by my daughter! Justice! Find the girl!
	She hath the stones upon her, and the ducats!"
Salerio	Why, all the boys in Venice follow him,
	Crying his stones, his daughter, and his ducats.
Solanio	Let good Antonio look he keep his day,
	Or he shall pay for this.
Salerio	Marry, well remember'd.
	I reason'd with a Frenchman yesterday, [27–34]
	Who told me, in the narrow seas that part
	The French and English, there miscarrièd
	A vessel of our country richly fraught: 30
	I thought upon Antonio when he told me,
	And wish'd in silence that it were not his.
Solanio	You were best to tell Antonio what you hear,
	Yet do not suddenly, for it may grieve him.
Salerio	A kinder gentleman treads not the earth.
	I saw Bassanio and Antonio part:
	Bassanio told him he would make some speed
	Of his return: he answer'd, "Do not so,
	Slubber not business for my sake, Bassanio,
	But stay the very riping of the time, 40
	And for the Jew's bond which he hath of me,
	Let it not enter in your mind of love:
	Be merry, and employ your chiefest thoughts
	To courtship, and such fair ostents of love
	As shall conveniently become you there."
	And even there, his eye being big with tears,
	Turning his face, he put his hand behind him,

39 **Slubber:** Perform carelessly
44 **ostents:** professions

	And with affection wondrous sensible	
	He wrung Bassanio's hand, and so they parted.	
Solanio	I think he only loves the world for him.	50
	I pray thee let us go and find him out,	
	And quicken his embracèd heaviness	
	With some delight or other.	
Salerio	Do we so. *Exeunt*	

Scene 9

[Scene 12]

Belmont. A room in Portia's house

Enter Nerissa and a servant

Nerissa	Quick, quick, I pray thee, draw the curtain straight;	
	The prince of Arragon hath ta'en his oath,	
	And comes to his election presently.	

Enter the Prince of Arragon, Portia, and their trains

Portia	Behold, there stand the caskets, noble prince;	
	If you choose that wherein I am contain'd,	
	Straight shall our nuptial rites be solemniz'd:	
	But if you fail, without more speech, my lord,	
	You must be gone from hence immediately.	
Arragon	I am enjoin'd by oath to observe three things:	
	First, never to unfold to any one	10
	Which casket 'twas I chose; next, if I fail	
	Of the right casket, never in my life	
	To woo a maid in way of marriage: lastly,	
	If I do fail in fortune of my choice,	
	Immediately to leave you, and be gone.	
Portia	To these injunctions every one doth swear	
	That come to hazard for my worthless self.	
Arragon	And so have I address'd me; fortune now	
	To my heart's hope! Gold, silver, and base lead.	
	"Who chooseth me, must give and hazard all he	
	hath."	20
	You shall look fairer ere I give or hazard.	
	What says the golden chest? Ha! Let me see:	
	"Who chooseth me, shall gain what many men desire."	
	What many men desire? That "many" may be meant	

1 **straight:** at once
3 **election:** choice

Benedict Campbell as the Prince of Arragon, with
Ernest Harrop and Brent Stait:
   "What's here? The portrait of a blinking idiot,
   Presenting me a schedule! I will read it.
   How much unlike art thou to Portia!
   How much unlike my hopes and my deservings!"

By the fool multitude, that choose by show,
Not learning more than the fond eye doth teach,
Which pries not to the interior, but, like the martlet,   [27–29]
Builds in the weather on the outward wall,
Even in the force and road of casualty.
I will not choose what many men desire,   30
Because I will not jump with common spirits,
And rank me with the barbarous multitudes.
Why then, to thee, thou silver treasure-house,
Tell me once more what title thou dost bear;
"Who chooseth me shall get as much as he deserves":
And well said too; for who shall go about
To cozen fortune, and be honourable
Without the stamp of merit? Let none presume
To wear an undeservèd dignity.
O, that estates, degrees, and offices   40
Were not deriv'd corruptly, and that clear honour
Were purchas'd by the merit of the wearer!
How many then should cover that stand bare!
How many be commanded that command!
How much low peasantry would then be glean'd
From the true seed of honour! And how much honour
Pick'd from the chaff and ruin of the times,
To be new-varnish'd! Well, but to my choice:
"Who chooseth me shall get as much as he deserves."
I will assume desert; give me a key for this,   50
And instantly unlock my fortunes here.
                               He opens the silver casket

Portia   (*aside*) Too long a pause for that which you find
                   there.

Arragon   What's here? The portrait of a blinking idiot,
               Presenting me a schedule! I will read it.
               How much unlike art thou to Portia!
               How much unlike my hopes and my deservings!
               "Who chooseth me, shall have as much as he
                   deserves"?
               Did I deserve no more than a fool's head?
               Is that my prize? Are my deserts no better?

Portia   To offend, and judge, are distinct offices,   60
               And of opposed natures.

---

27 **martlet:** a bird (swift) that builds its nest in exposed places
31 **jump:** agree; join
37 **cozen:** cheat
54 **schedule:** scroll

Arragon   What is here?

    (*Reads*) "The fire seven times tried this,   [62–64]
              Seven times tried that judgement is,
              That did never choose amiss.
              Some there be that shadows kiss,
              Such have but a shadow's bliss:
              There be fools alive, I wis,
              Silver'd o'er, and so was this.
              Take what wife you will to bed,
              I will ever be your head: 70
              So be gone, you are sped."

    Still more I shall appear
    By the time I linger here:
    With one fool's head I came to woo,
    But I go away with two.
    Sweet, adieu; I'll keep my oath,
    Patiently to bear my wroth.

                       Exeunt Arragon and train

Portia   Thus hath the candle sing'd the moth.
    O, these deliberate fools! When they do choose,
    They have the wisdom by their wit to lose.   80

Nerissa   The ancient saying is no heresy,
    Hanging and wiving goes by destiny.

Portia   Come, draw the curtain, Nerissa.   [83]

Enter a servant

Servant   Where is my lady?

Portia   Here: what would my lord?

Servant   Madam, there is alighted at your gate
    A young Venetian, one that comes before
    To signify the approaching of his lord,
    From whom he bringeth sensible regrets;
    To wit, besides commends and courteous breath,
    Gifts of rich value; yet I have not seen   90
    So likely an ambassador of love.
    A day in April never came so sweet
    To show how costly summer was at hand,
    As this fore-spurrer comes before his lord.

Portia   No more, I pray thee; I am half afeard
    Thou wilt say anon he is some kin to thee,

---

68 **silver'd o'er:** with silver hair (appearing wise)
88 **sensible regreets:** tangible tokens of greeting
89 **commends:** compliments

	Thou spend'st such high-day wit in praising him.	
	Come, come, Nerissa, for I long to see	
	Quick Cupid's post that comes so mannerly.	
Nerissa	Bassanio, lord Love, if thy will it be!	100

Exeunt

---

97   **high-day:** holiday

Shylock:
　　"... I am a Jew. Hath not a Jew eyes,
　　hath not a Jew hands, organs, dimensions,
　　sense, affections, passions . . .? If you
　　prick us, do we not bleed?"

Act Third

Scene 1

[Scene 13]

Venice. A street

Enter Solanio and Salerio

Solanio   Now, what news on the Rialto?

Salerio   Why, yet it lives there uncheck'd, that Antonio
hath a ship of rich lading wreck'd on the narrow
seas; the Goodwins I think they call the place, a
very dangerous flat, and fatal, where the carcases
of many a tall ship lie buried, as they say, if my
gossip Report be an honest woman of her word.

Solanio   I would she were as lying a gossip in that as ever   [8–10]
knapp'd ginger, or made her neighbours believe
she wept for the death of a third husband: but it is   10
true, without any slips of prolixity, or crossing the
plain highway of talk, that the good Antonio, the
honest Antonio, – O that I had a title good enough
to keep his name company –

Salerio   Come, the full stop.

Solanio   Ha! What sayest thou? Why, the end is, he hath
lost a ship.

Salerio   I would it might prove the end of his losses.

Solanio   Let me say "amen" betimes, lest the devil cross my
prayer, for here he comes in the likeness of a Jew.   20

Enter Shylock

    How now, Shylock, what news among the merchants?

Shylock   You knew, none so well, none so well as you, of my
daughter's flight.

---

  2 **uncheck'd:** uncontradicted
  9 **knapp'd:** chewed loudly
15 **full stop:** a term used in training horses

Salerio	That's certain; I, for my part, knew the tailor that made the wings she flew withal.
Solanio	And Shylock, for his own part, knew the bird was fledg'd; and then it is the complexion of them all to leave the dam.
Shylock	She is damn'd for it.
Salerio	That's certain, if the devil may be her judge. 30
Shylock	My own flesh and blood to rebel!
Solanio	Out upon it, old carrion! Rebels it at these years?
Shylock	I say my daughter is my flesh and blood.
Salerio	There is more difference between thy flesh and hers, than between jet and ivory, more between your bloods, than there is between red wine and rhenish. But tell us, do you hear whether Antonio have had any loss at sea or no?
Shylock	There I have another bad match, a bankrupt, a prodigal, who dare scarce show his head on the 40 Rialto, a beggar, that was used to come so smug upon the mart; let him look to his bond; he was wont to call me usurer, let him look to his bond; he was wont to lend money for a Christian curtsy, let him look to his bond.
Salerio	Why, I am sure, if he forfeit, thou wilt not take his flesh. What's that good for?
Shylock	To bait fish withal, if it will feed nothing else, it will feed my revenge. He hath disgrac'd me, and hinder'd me half a million, laugh'd at my losses, 50 mock'd at my gains, scorned my nation, thwarted my bargains, cool'd my friends, heated mine enemies, and what's reason? I am a Jew. Hath not a Jew eyes, hath not a Jew hands, organs, dimensions, sense, affections, passions, fed with the same food, hurt with the same weapons, subject to the same diseases, healed by the same means, warmed and cooled by the same winter and summer as a Christian is? If you prick us, do we not bleed? If you tickle us do we not laugh; if you poison us do we not die; 60 and if you wrong us, shall we not revenge? If we are like you in the rest, we will resemble you in that. If a Jew wrong a Christian, what is his humility? Revenge. If a Christian wrong a Jew, what should his sufferance be by Christian example? Why, re- venge. The villany you teach me I will execute, and

27 **complexion:** habit
36 **rhenish:** Rhine wine
39 **match:** bargain

	it shall go hard but I will better the instruction.
Enter a servant	
Servant	Gentlemen, my master Antonio is at his house, and desires to speak with you both.
Salerio	We have been up and down to seek him.

70

Enter Tubal

Solanio	Here comes another of the tribe; a third cannot be match'd, unless the devil himself turn Jew.
	Exeunt Solanio, Salerio, and servant
Shylock	How now, Tubal, what news from Genoa? Hast thou found my daughter?
Tubal	I often came where I did hear of her, but cannot find her.
Shylock	Why, there, there, there, there! A diamond gone, cost me two thousand ducats in Frankfort! The curse never fell upon our nation till now; I never felt it till now, two thousand ducats in that, and other precious, precious jewels. I would my daughter were dead at my foot, and the jewels in her car! Would she were hears'd at my foot, and the ducats in her coffin! No news of them? Why, so: – and I know not what's spent in the search: why, thou loss upon loss! The thief gone with so much, and so much to find the thief, and no satis-faction, no revenge, nor no ill luck stirring but what lights o' my shoulders, no sighs but o' my breathing, no tears but o' my shedding.
Tubal	Yes, other men have ill luck too; Antonio, as I heard in Genoa, –
Shylock	What, what, what? Ill luck, ill luck?
Tubal	Hath an argosy cast away, coming from Tripolis.
Shylock	I thank God, I thank God! Is it true, is it true?
Tubal	I spoke with some of the sailors that escaped the wreck.
Shylock	I thank thee, good Tubal: good news, good news! Ha, ha! Here in Genoa.
Tubal	Your daughter spent in Genoa, as I heard, one night fourscore ducats.
Shylock	Thou stick'st a dagger in me, I shall never see my gold again: fourscore ducats at a sitting! Fourscore ducats!
Tubal	There came divers of Antonio's creditors in my com-

80

90

[99]

100

**Bassanio with the three caskets, held by Susan
Morgan, Caro Coltman, and Janet MacDonald:**
"... Let me choose,
For as I am, I live upon the rack."

	pany to Venice, that swear he cannot choose but break.
Shylock	I am very glad of it; I'll plague him, I'll torture him: I am glad of it.
Tubal	One of them showed me a ring that he had of your daughter for a monkey.
Shylock	Out upon her! Thou torturest me, Tubal, it was my turquoise, I had it of Leah when I was a bachelor: I would not have given it for a wilderness of monkeys.
Tubal	But Antonio is certainly undone.
Shylock	Nay, that's true, that's very true. Go, Tubal, fee me an officer, bespeak him a fortnight before, I will have the heart of him if he forfeit, for were he out of Venice I can make what merchandise I will. Go, Tubal, and meet me at our synagogue; go, good Tubal, at our synagogue, Tubal. *Exeunt*

110

120

INTERVAL

Scene 2

[Scene 14]

Belmont. A room in Portia's house

Enter Bassanio, Portia, Gratiano, Nerissa, and Attendants

Portia	I pray you tarry, pause a day or two
	Before you hazard, for, in choosing wrong,
	I lose your company; therefore forbear a while.
	There's something tells me, but it is not love,
	I would not lose you, and you know yourself,
	Hate counsels not in such a quality.
	But lest you should not understand me well, –
	And yet a maiden hath no tongue, but thought, –
	I would detain you here some month or two
	Before you venture for me. I could teach you
	How to choose right, but then I am forsworn;
	So will I never be, so may you miss me,
	But if you do, you'll make me wish a sin,
	That I had been forsworn. Beshrew your eyes,
	They have o'er-look'd me and divided me,

10

---

107 **break:** become bankrupt
14 **Beshrew:** May evil befall
15 **o'er-looked:** bewitched

<pre>
                One half of me is yours, the other half yours,
                Mine own, I would say; but if mine, then yours,
                And so all yours! O, these naughty times
                Puts bars between the owners and their rights,
                And so, though yours, not yours. Prove it so,   20
                Let fortune go to hell for it, not I.
                I speak too long, but 'tis to peize the time,
                To eke it, and to draw it out in length,
                To stay you from election.
Bassanio   Let me choose,
                For as I am, I live upon the rack.
Portia   Upon the rack, Bassanio? Then confess
                What treason there is mingled with your love.
Bassanio   None but that ugly treason of mistrust,
                Which makes me fear the enjoying of my love:
                There may as well be amity and life   30
                'Tween snow and fire, as treason and my love.
Portia   Ay, but I fear you speak upon the rack,
                Where men enforced do speak any thing.
Bassanio   Promise me life, and I'll confess the truth.
Portia   Well then, confess and live.
Bassanio   "Confess," and "love,"
                Had been the very sum of my confession:
                O happy torment, when my torturer
                Doth teach me answers for deliverance!
                But let me to my fortune and the caskets.
Portia   Away, then! I am lock'd in one of them: 40
                If you do love me, you will find me out.
                Nerissa and the rest, stand all aloof,
                Let music sound while he doth make his choice,
                Then, if he lose, he makes a swan-like end,
                Fading in music: that the comparison
                May stand more proper, my eye shall be the stream
                And watery death-bed for him. He may win,
                And what is music then? Then music is
                Even as the flourish, when true subjects bow
                To a new-crownèd monarch: such it is,   50
                As are those dulcet sounds in break of day,
                That creep into the dreaming bridegroom's ear,
                And summon him to marriage. Now he goes
                With no less presence, but with much more love,
                Than young Alcides, when he did redeem
                The virgin tribute, paid by howling Troy
                To the sea-monster: I stand for sacrifice;
</pre>

22 **peize:** weigh down (put brakes on)
55 **Alcides:** Hercules

The rest aloof are the Dardanian wives,
With bleared visages come forth to view
The issue of the exploit. Go, Hercules!   60
Live thou, I live: with much much more dismay
I view the fight than thou that mak'st the fray.

A song, the whilst Bassanio comments on the caskets
to himself

    Tell me where is fancy bred,
    Or in the heart or in the head,
    How begot, how nourished?
      Reply, reply.
    It is engender'd in the eyes,
    With gazing fed, and fancy dies
    In the cradle where it lies.
      Let us all ring fancy's knell;   70
      I'll begin it, – Ding, dong, bell.
    Ding, dong, bell.

Bassanio   So may the outward shows be least themselves:
The world is still deceiv'd with ornament;
In law, what plea so tainted and corrupt,
But, being season'd with a gracious voice,
Obscures the show of evil? In religion,
What damnèd error, but some sober brow
Will bless it, and approve it with a text,
Hiding the grossness with fair ornament?   80
There is no vice so simple, but assumes
Some mark of virtue on his outward parts:
How many cowards whose hearts are all as false
As stairs of sand wear yet upon their chins
The beards of Hercules and frowning Mars,
Who, inward search'd, have livers white as milk,
And these assume but valour's excrement
To render them redoubted! Look on beauty,
And you shall see 'tis purchas'd by the weight,
Which therein works a miracle in nature,   90
Making them lightest that wear most of it:
So are those crispèd snaky golden locks
Which make such wanton gambols with the wind
Upon supposèd fairness, often known
To be the dowry of a second head,
The skull that bred them in the sepulchre.
Thus ornament is but the guilèd shore
To a most dangerous sea; the beauteous scarf

---

58 **Dardanian:** Trojan   92 **crispèd:** curled (like hair)
63 **fancy:** love   97 **guiled:** guileful
87 **excrement:** outgrowth

Gratiano, Nerissa, and Portia's Lady
learn what Bassanio's casket holds:
  "What find I here?
  Fair Portia's counterfeit! What demi-god
  Hath come so near creation?"

Veiling an Indian beauty; in a word,
The seeming truth which cunning times put on   100
To entrap the wisest. Therefore, thou gaudy gold,
Hard food for Midas, I will none of thee,
Nor none of thee, thou pale and common drudge
'Tween man and man: but thou, thou meagre lead,
Which rather threaten'st than dost promise aught,
Thy plainness moves me more than eloquence,
And here choose I, joy be the consequence!

Portia   (aside) How all the other passions fleet to air,
As doubtful thoughts, and rash-embrac'd despair,
And shudd'ring fear, and green-eyed jealousy!   110
O love, be moderate, allay thy ecstasy,
In measure rain thy joy, scant this excess!
I feel too much thy blessing, make it less,
For fear I surfeit!

Bassanio   What find I here?

Opening the leaden casket

Fair Portia's counterfeit! What demi-god
Hath come so near creation? Move these eyes?
Or whether, riding on the balls of mine,
Seem they in motion? Here are sever'd lips
Parted with sugar breath; so sweet a bar
Should sunder such sweet friends. Here in her hairs   120
The painter plays the spider, and hath woven
A golden mesh to entrap the hearts of men
Faster than gnats in cobwebs; but her eyes, –
How could he see to do them? Having made one,
Methinks it should have power to steal both his
And leave itself unfurnish'd. Yet look how far
The substance of my praise doth wrong this shadow
In underprizing it, so far this shadow
Doth limp behind the substance. Here's the scroll,
The continent and summary of my fortune.   130

(Reads)   "You that choose not by the view,
Chance as fair, and choose as true!
Since this fortune falls to you,
Be content, and seek no new.
If you be well pleas'd with this,
And hold your fortune for your bliss,
Turn you where your lady is,
And claim her with a loving kiss."

---

118   **sever'd:** open
127   **shadow:** portrait
130   **continent:** contents; container

	A gentle scroll. Fair lady, by your leave,	
	I come by note to give, and to receive,	140
	Like one of two contending in a prize,	
	That thinks he hath done well in people's eyes;	
	Hearing applause and universal shout,	
	Giddy in spirit, still gazing in a doubt	
	Whether those peals of praise be his or no,	
	So, thrice-fair lady, stand I, even so,	
	As doubtful whether what I see be true,	
	Until confirm'd, sign'd, ratified by you.	
Portia	You see me, Lord Bassanio, where I stand,	
	Such as I am; though for myself alone	150

Portia   You see me, Lord Bassanio, where I stand,
Such as I am; though for myself alone   150
I would not be ambitious in my wish
To wish myself much better, yet for you,
I would be trebled twenty times myself,
A thousand times more fair, ten thousand times
More rich;
That only to stand high in your account,
I might in virtues, beauties, livings, friends,
Exceed account; but the full sum of me
Is sum of something; which, to term in gross,
Is an unlesson'd girl, unschool'd, unpractised,   160
Happy in this, she is not yet so old
But she may learn; happier than this,
She is not bred so dull but she can learn;
Happiest of all, is that her gentle spirit
Commits itself to yours to be directed,
As from her lord, her governor, her king.
Myself, and what is mine, to you and yours
Is now converted: but now I was the lord
Of this fair mansion, master of my servants,
Queen o'er myself; and even now, but now,   170
This house, these servants, and this same myself,
Are yours, my lord's: I give them with this ring,
Which when you part from, lose, or give away,
Let it presage the ruin of your love,
And be my vantage to exclaim on you.
Bassanio   Madam, you have bereft me of all words,
Only my blood speaks to you in my veins,
And there is such confusion in my powers,
As, after some oration fairly spoke
By a beloved prince, there doth appear   180
Among the buzzing pleasèd multitude;

---

141   **prize:** contest
157   **livings:** property
159   **to term in gross:** to sum up

	Where every something, being blent together,	
	Turns to a wild of nothing, save of joy,	
	Express'd, and not express'd. But when this ring	
	Parts from this finger, then parts life from hence,	
	O, then be bold to say Bassanio's dead!	
Nerissa	My lord and lady, it is now our time,	
	That have stood by and seen our wishes prosper,	
	To cry "good joy, good joy, my lord and lady!"	
Gratiano	My lord Bassanio, and my gentle lady,	190
	I wish you all the joy that you can wish;	
	For I am sure you can wish none from me:	
	And when your honours mean to solemnize	
	The bargain of your faith, I do beseech you,	
	Even at that time I may be married too.	
Bassanio	With all my heart, so thou canst get a wife.	
Gratiano	I thank your lordship, you have got me one.	
	My eyes, my lord, can look a swift as yours:	
	You saw the mistress, I beheld the maid;	
	You lov'd, I lov'd for intermission;	200
	No more pertains to me, my lord, than you.	
	Your fortune stood upon the caskets there,	
	And so did mine too, as the matter falls;	
	For wooing here until I sweat again,	
	And swearing till my very roof was dry	
	With oaths of love, at last, if promise last,	
	I got a promise of this fair one here	
	To have her love; provided that your fortune	
	Achiev'd her mistress.	
Portia	Is this true, Nerissa?	
Nerissa	Madam, it is, so you stand pleas'd withal.	210
Bassanio	And do you, Gratiano, mean good faith?	
Gratiano	Yes, faith, my lord.	
Bassanio	Our feast shall be much honoured in your marriage.	
Gratiano	We'll play with them the first boy for a thousand ducats.	
Nerissa	What, and stake down?	
Gratiano	No, we shall ne'er win at that sport, and stake down.	
	But who comes here? Lorenzo and his infidel?	
	What, and my old Venetian friend Salerio?	

Enter Lorenzo, Jessica, and Salerio, a messenger from Venice

Bassanio	Lorenzo and Salerio, welcome hither,	220
	If that the youth of my new interest here	
	Have power to bid you welcome. By your leave,	

182	**blent:** blended	205	**roof:** (of his mouth)
200	**intermission:** to pass the time	216	**stake down:** wager

	I bid my very friends and countrymen,	
	Sweet Portia, welcome.	
Portia	So do I, my lord,	
	They are entirely welcome.	
Lorenzo	I thank your honour; for my part, my lord,	
	My purpose was not to have seen you here,	
	But meeting with Salerio by the way,	
	He did entreat me, past all saying nay,	
	To come with him along.	
Salerio	I did, my lord,	230
	And I have reason for it; Signior Antonio	
	Commends him to you. *Gives Bassanio a letter*	
Bassanio	Ere I ope his letter,	
	I pray you tell me how my good friend doth.	
Salerio	Not sick, my lord, unless it be in mind,	
	Nor well, unless in mind: his letter there	
	Will show you his estate.	
	Bassanio opens the letter	
Gratiano	Nerissa, cheer yon stranger, bid her welcome.	
	Your hand, Salerio, what's the news from Venice?	
	How doth that royal merchant, good Antonio?	
	I know he will be glad of our success,	240
	We are the Jasons, we have won the fleece.	
Salerio	I would you had won the fleece that he hath lost.	
Portia	There are some shrewd contents in yon same paper,	
	That steals the colour from Bassanio's cheek,	
	Some dear friend dead, else nothing in the world	
	Could turn so much the constitution	
	Of any constant man. What, worse and worse?	
	With leave, Bassanio, I am half yourself,	
	And I must freely have the half of anything	
	That this same paper brings you.	
Bassanio	O sweet Portia,	250
	Here are a few of the unpleasant'st words	
	That ever blotted paper! Gentle lady,	
	When I did first impart my love to you,	
	I freely told you all the wealth I had	
	Ran in my veins, I was a gentleman,	
	And then I told you true: and yet, dear lady,	
	Rating myself at nothing, you shall see	
	How much I was a braggart; when I told you	
	My state was nothing, I should then have told you	
	That I was worse than nothing; for, indeed,	260
	I have engag'd myself to a dear friend,	

232 **ope:** open
243 **shrewd:** biting, bad

Salerio:
    "The Duke himself, and the magnificoes
    Of greatest port, have all persuaded with him,
    But none can drive him from the envious plea
    Of forfeiture, of justice, and his bond."

	Engag'd my friend to his mere enemy,	
	To feed my means. Here is a letter, lady,	
	The paper as the body of my friend,	
	And every word in it a gaping wound	
	Issuing life-blood. But is it true, Salerio?	
	Hath all his ventures fail'd? What, not one hit?	
	From Tripolis, from Mexico, and England,	
	From Lisbon, Barbary, and India,	
	And not one vessel 'scape the dreadful touch	270
	Of merchant-marring rocks?	
Salerio	Not one, my lord.	
	Besides, it should appear, that if he had	
	The present money to discharge the Jew,	
	He would not take it: never did I know	
	A creature that did bear the shape of man	
	So keen and greedy to confound a man.	
	He plies the Duke at morning and at night,	
	And doth impeach the freedom of the state	
	If they deny him justice: twenty merchants,	
	The Duke himself, and the magnificoes	280
	Of greatest port, have all persuaded with him,	
	But none can drive him from the envious plea	
	Of forfeiture, of justice, and his bond.	
Jessica	When I was with him, I have heard him swear	
	To Tubal and to Chus, his countrymen,	
	That he would rather have Antonio's flesh	
	Than twenty times the value of the sum	
	That he did owe him: and I know, my lord,	
	If law, authority, and power deny not,	
	It will go hard with poor Antonio.	290
Portia	Is it your dear friend that is thus in trouble?	
Bassanio	The dearest friend to me, the kindest man,	
	The best-condition'd and unwearied spirit	
	In doing courtesies; and one in whom	
	The ancient Roman honour more appears	
	Than any that draws breath in Italy.	
Portia	What sum owes he the Jew?	
Bassanio	For me three thousand ducats.	
Portia	What, no more?	
	Pay him six thousand, and deface the bond;	
	Double six thousand, and then treble that,	300
	Before a friend of this description	
	Shall lose a hair through Bassanio's fault.	

---

262 **Engag'd:** Pledged	281 **persuaded:** pleaded
mere: out-and-out, clear	282 **envious:** malicious
280 **magnificoes:** nobles	299 **deface:** cancel

First go with me to church, and call me wife,
And then away to Venice to your friend;
For never shall you lie by Portia's side
With an unquiet soul. You shall have gold
To pay the petty debt twenty times over.
When it is paid, bring your true friend along;
My maid Nerissa and myself meantime
Will live as maids and widows. Come, away,   310
For you shall hence upon your wedding-day:
Bid your friends welcome, show a merry cheer,
Since you are dear bought, I will love you dear.
But let me hear the letter of your friend.

Bassanio (*reads*) "Sweet Bassanio, my ships have all miscarried,
my creditors grow cruel, my estate is very low, my
bond to the Jew is forfeit, and since in paying it, it
is impossible I should live, all debts are clear'd between you and I, if I might but see you at my death:
notwithstanding, use your pleasure; if your love   320
do not persuade you to come, let not my letter."

Portia O love, dispatch all business, and be gone!

Bassanio Since I have your good leave to go away,
  I will make haste: but, till I come again,
No bed shall e'er be guilty of my stay.
  Nor rest be interposer 'twixt us twain.   *Exeunt*

Scene 3

[Scene 15]

Venice. A street

Enter Shylock, Solanio, Antonio, and Gaoler

Shylock Gaoler, look to him, tell not me of mercy;
  This is the fool that lent out money gratis:
  Gaoler, look to him.

Antonio   Hear me yet, good Shylock.

Shylock I'll have my bond, speak not against my bond,
  I have sworn an oath, that I will have my bond:
  Thou call'dst me dog before thou hadst a cause,
  But, since I am a dog, beware my fangs;
  The Duke shall grant me justice, I do wonder,

311 **hence:** go hence

71

Shylock:
"I have sworn an oath, that I'll have my bond:
Thou call'dst me dog before thou hadst a cause,
But, since I am a dog, beware my fangs."

	Thou naughty gaoler, that thou are so fond
	To come abroad with him at his request.	10
Antonio	I pray thee hear me speak.
Shylock	I'll have my bond. I will not hear thee speak,
	I'll have my bond, and therefore speak no more.
	I'll not be made a soft and dull-eyed fool,
	To shake the head, relent, and sigh, and yield
	To Christian intercessors. Follow not,
	I'll have no speaking, I will have my bond. *Exit*
Solanio	It is the most impenetrable cur
	That ever kept with men.
Antonio	Let him alone,
	I'll follow him no more with bootless prayers.	20
	He seeks my life, his reason well I know:
	I oft deliver'd from his forfeitures
	Many that have at times made moan to me,
	Therefore he hates me.
Solanio	I am sure the Duke
	Will never grant this forfeiture to hold.
Antonio	The Duke cannot deny the course of law:
	For the commodity that strangers have
	With us in Venice, if it be denied,
	Will much impeach the justice of the state,
	Since that the trade and profit of the city	30
	Consisteth of all nations. Therefore, go;
	These griefs and losses have so bated me
	That I shall hardly spare a pound of flesh
	To-morrow, to my bloody creditor.
	Well, gaoler, on; pray God Bassanio come	[35]
	To see me pay his debt, and then I care not!

Exeunt

Scene 4

Belmont. A room in Portia's house

Enter Portia, Nerissa, Lorenzo, Jessica, and Balthasar

Lorenzo	Madam, although I speak it in your presence,
	You have a noble and a true conceit
	Of god-like amity, which appears most strongly

9	**naughty:** worthless		29	**impeach:** discredit
	fond: foolish		32	**bated:** reduced
22	**forfeitures:** foreclosures, liabilities (to him)		2	**conceit:** conception

	In bearing thus the absence of your lord.	
	But if you knew to whom you show this honour,	
	How true a gentleman you send relief,	
	How dear a lover of my lord your husband,	
	I know you would be prouder of the work	
	Than customary bounty can enforce you.	
Portia	I never did repent for doing good,	10
	Nor shall not now: for in companions	
	That do converse and waste the time together,	
	Whose souls do bear an equal yoke of love,	
	There must be needs a like proportion	
	Of lineaments, of manners, and of spirit;	
	Which makes me think that this Antonio,	
	Being the bosom lover of my lord,	
	Must needs be like my lord. If it be so,	
	How little is the cost I have bestow'd	
	In purchasing the semblance of my soul	20
	From out the state of hellish cruelty!	
	This comes too near the praising of myself,	
	Therefore no more of it: hear other things.	
	Lorenzo, I commit into your hands	
	The husbandry and manage of my house,	
	Until my lord's return: for mine own part,	
	I have toward heaven breath'd a secret vow,	
	To live in prayer and contemplation,	
	Only attended by Nerissa here,	
	Until her husband and my lord's return:	30
	There is a monastery two miles off,	
	And there we will abide. I do desire you	
	Not to deny this imposition,	
	The which my love and some necessity	
	Now lays upon you.	
Lorenzo	Madam, with all my heart,	
	I shall obey you in all fair commands.	
Portia	My people do already know my mind,	
	And will acknowledge you and Jessica	
	In place of Lord Bassanio and myself.	
	So fare you well till we shall meet again.	40
Lorenzo	Fair thoughts and happy hours attend on you!	
Jessica	I wish your ladyship all heart's content.	
Portia	I thank you for your wish, and am well pleas'd	
	To wish it back on you: fare you well, Jessica.	

Exeunt Jessica and Lorenzo

---

15 **lineaments:** characteristics
37 **people:** servants

Portia speaks to Nerissa as one of her Ladies listens:
      ". . . I'll hold thee any wager,
      When we are both accoutred like young men,
      I'll prove the prettier fellow of the two."

Now, Balthasar,
As I have ever found thee honest-true,
So let me find thee still: take this same letter,
And use thou all the endeavour of a man,
In speed to Padua, see thou render this
Into my cousin's hand, Doctor Bellario,   50
And look what notes and garments he doth give thee,
Bring them, I pray thee, with imagin'd speed
Unto the tranect, to the common ferry
Which trades to Venice; waste no time in words,
But get thee gone, I shall be there before thee.

Balthasar   Madam, I go with all convenient speed.   *Exit*

Portia   Come on, Nerissa, I have work in hand
That you yet know not of; we'll see our husbands
Before they think of us.

Nerissa   Shall they see us?

Portia   They shall, Nerissa; but in such a habit,   60
That they shall think we are accomplishèd
With that we lack; I'll hold thee any wager,
When we are both accoutred like young men,
I'll prove the prettier fellow of the two.
And wear my dagger with the braver grace,
And speak between the change of man and boy,
With a reed voice, and turn two mincing steps
Into a manly stride; and speak of frays   [68–76]
Like a fine bragging youth; and tell quaint lies
How honourable ladies sought my love,   70
Which I denying, they fell sick and died;
I could not do withal: then I'll repent,
And wish, for all that, that I had not kill'd them;
And twenty of these puny lies I'll tell,
That men shall swear I have discontinued school
Above a twelvemonth: I have within my mind
A thousand raw tricks of these bragging Jacks,
Which I will practise.

Nerissa   Why, shall we turn to men?

Portia   Fie, what a question's that,
If thou wert near a lewd interpreter!   80
But come, I'll tell thee all my whole device
When I am in my coach, which stays for us
At the park-gate; and therefore haste away,
For we must measure twenty miles to-day.   *Exeunt*

---

52 **imagin'd:** all imaginable
53 **tranect:** possibly traject, meaning ferry

Scene 5

The same. A garden
Enter Launcelot and Jessica

Launcelot Yes truly, for look you, the sins of the father are to
be laid upon the children; therefore, I promise you,
I fear you. I was always plain with you, and so now
I speak my agitation of the matter: therefore be o'
good cheer, for truly I think you are damn'd, there
is but one hope in it that can do you any good, and
that is but a kind of bastard hope neither.

Jessica And what hope is that, I pray thee?

Launcelot Marry, you may partly hope that your father got you
not, that you are not the Jew's daughter.   10

Jessica That were a kind of bastard hope indeed, so the sins
of my mother should be visited upon me.

Launcelot Truly then I fear you are damn'd both by father and
mother: thus when I shun Scylla your father, I fall
into Charybdis your mother; well, you are gone both
ways.

Jessica I shall be sav'd by my husband, he hath made me a
Christian.

Launcelot Truly the more to blame he, we were Christians
enow before, e'en as many as could well live one by   20
another: this making of Christians will raise the
price of hogs, if we grow all to be pork-eaters, we   [22]
shall not shortly have a rasher on the coals for
money.

Enter Lorenzo

Jessica I'll tell my husband, Launcelot, what you say: here
he comes.

Lorenzo I shall grow jealous of you shortly, Launcelot, if you
thus get my wife into corners!

Jessica Nay, you need not fear us, Lorenzo, Launcelot and I
are out; he tells me flatly there's no mercy for me in   30
heaven, because I am a Jew's daughter: and he says
you are no good member of the commonwealth, for
in converting Jews to Christians, you raise the price
of pork.

Lorenzo I shall answer that better to the commonwealth   [35–44]
than you can the getting up of the negro's belly:

---

14 **Scylla:** and Charybdis (line 15), legendary monsters guarding
the strait between Italy and Sicily
20 **enow:** enough

Lorenzo holds Jessica's hand as he addresses Launcelot:
   "I shall grow jealous of you shortly, Launcelot,
   if you thus get my wife into corners!"

	the Moor is with child by you, Launcelot.	
Launcelot	It is much that the Moor should be more than	
	reason: but if she be less than an honest woman,	
	she is indeed more than I took her for.	40
Lorenzo	How every fool can play upon the word! I think	
	the best grace of wit will shortly turn into silence,	
	and discourse grow commendable in none only but	
	parrots. Go in, sirrah, bid them prepare for dinner.	
Launcelot	That is done, sir; they have all stomachs.	
Lorenzo	Goodly Lord, what a wit-snapper are you! Then	[46-52]
	bid them prepare dinner.	
Launcelot	That is done too, sir, only "cover" is the word.	
Lorenzo	Will you cover, then, sir?	
Launcelot	Not so, sir, neither; I know my duty.	50
Lorenzo	Yet more quarrelling with occasion! Wilt thou	
	show the whole wealth of thy wit in an instant? I	
	pray thee understand a plain man in his plain mean-	
	ing: go to thy fellows, bid them cover the table,	
	serve in the meat, and we will come in to dinner.	
Launcelot	For the table, sir, it shall be serv'd in, for the meat,	
	sir, it shall be cover'd, for your coming in to dinner,	
	sir, why, let it be as humours and conceits shall	
	govern. *Exit*	
Lorenzo	O dear discretion, how his words are suited!	[60-65]
	The fool hath planted in his memory	
	An army of good words, and I do know	
	A many fools, that stand in better place,	
	Garnish'd like him, that for a tricksy word	
	Defy the matter. How cheer'st thou, Jessica?	
	And now, good sweet, say thy opinion,	
	How dost thou like the Lord Bassanio's wife?	
Jessica	Past all expressing. It is very meet	
	The Lord Bassanio live an upright life,	
	For, having such a blessing in his lady,	70
	He finds the joys of heaven here on earth,	
	And if on earth he do not merit it,	
	In reason he should never come to heaven.	
	Why, if two gods should play some heavenly match,	
	And on the wager lay two earthly women,	
	And Portia one, there must be something else	
	Pawn'd with the other; for the poor rude world	
	Hath not her fellow.	
Lorenzo	Even such a husband	
	Hast thou of me as she is for a wife.	

65 **defy the matter:** evade the point
77 **Pawn'd with:** Added to the value of

Jessica	Nay, but ask my opinion too of that.	80
Lorenzo	I will anon; first let us go to dinner.	
Jessica	Nay, let me praise you while I have a stomach.	
Lorenzo	No, pray thee, let it serve for table-talk,	
	Then, howsoe'er thou speak'st, 'mong other things	
	I shall digest it.	
Jessica	Well, I'll set you forth.	*Exeunt*

82   **stomach:** inclination

Act Fourth

Scene 1

[Scene 18]

Venice. A court of justice

Enter the Duke, the Magnificoes, Antonio, Bassanio, Gratiano,
Salerio, and others

Duke	What, is Antonio here?
Antonio	Ready, so please your Grace.
Duke	I am sorry for thee, thou art come to answer
	A stony adversary, an inhuman wretch,
	Uncapable of pity, void and empty
	From any dram of mercy.
Antonio	I have heard
	Your Grace hath ta'en great pains to qualify
	His rigorous course; but since he stands obdurate,
	And that no lawful means can carry me
	Out of his envy's reach, I do oppose 10
	My patience to his fury, and am arm'd
	To suffer with a quietness of spirit,
	The very tyranny and rage of his.
Duke	Go one and call the Jew into the court.
Salerio	He is ready at the door; he comes, my lord.

Enter Shylock

Duke	Make room, and let him stand before our face.
	Shylock, the world thinks, and I think so too,
	That thou but leadest this fashion of thy malice
	To the last hour of act, and then 'tis thought
	Thou'lt show thy mercy and remorse more strange 20
	Than is thy strange apparent cruelty;

---

18 **fashion:** pretence
20 **remorse:** compassion   **strange:** remarkable

	And where thou now exacts the penalty,	
	Which is a pound of this poor merchant's flesh,	
	Thou wilt not only lose the forfeiture,	
	But, touch'd with human gentleness and love,	
	Forgive a moiety of the principal,	
	Glancing an eye of pity on his losses,	
	That have of late so huddled on his back,	
	Enow to press a royal merchant down,	
	And pluck commiseration of his state	30
	From brassy bosoms and rough hearts of flints,	
	From stubborn Turks, and Tartars never train'd	
	To offices of tender courtesy.	
	We all expect a gentle answer, Jew.	
Shylock	I have possess'd your Grace of what I purpose,	
	And by our holy Sabbath have I sworn	
	To have the due and forfeit of my bond.	
	If you deny it, let the danger light	
	Upon your charter and your city's freedom.	
	You'll ask me why I rather choose to have	40
	A weight of carrion-flesh than to receive	
	Three thousand ducats: I'll not answer that:	
	But say it is my humour; is it answer'd?	
	What if my house be troubled with a rat,	
	And I be pleas'd to give ten thousand ducats	
	To have it ban'd? What, are you answer'd yet?	
	Some men there are love not a gaping pig;	
	Some that are mad if they behold a cat;	
	And others, when the bagpipe sings i' the nose,	
	Cannot contain their urine: for affection,	50
	Master of passion, sways it to the mood	
	Of what it likes or loathes. Now for your answer;	
	As there is no firm reason to be render'd	
	Why he cannot abide a gaping pig;	
	Why he a harmless necessary cat;	
	Why he a woollen bag-pipe; but of force	
	Must yield to such inevitable shame	
	As to offend, himself being offended;	
	So can I give no reason, nor I will not,	
	More than a lodg'd hate and a certain loathing	60
	I bear Antonio, that I follow thus	
	A losing suit against him. Are you answer'd?	

26 **moiety:** portion
29 **royal:** i.e., with the resources of a king
35 **possess'd:** informed
43 **humour:** whim
46 **ban'd:** poisoned
47 **gaping pig:** roasted boar's head, served with its mouth open

Shylock:
    "The pound of flesh which I demand of him
    Is dearly bought, is mine, and I will have it."

Bassanio	This is no answer, thou unfeeling man,
	To excuse the current of thy cruelty.
Shylock	I am not bound to please thee with my answers.
Bassanio	Do all men kill the things they do not love?
Shylock	Hates any man the thing he would not kill?
Bassanio	Every offence is not a hate at first.
Shylock	What, wouldst thou have a serpent sting thee twice?
Antonio	I pray you, think you question with the Jew?
	You may as well go stand upon the beach,

71

And bid the main flood bate his usual height;
You may as well use question with the wolf,
Why he hath made the ewe bleat for the lamb;
You may as well forbid the mountain pines
To wag their high tops, and to make no noise,
When they are fretten with the gusts of heaven;
You may as well do any thing most hard,
As seek to soften that – than which what's harder? –
His Jewish heart. Therefore, I do beseech you,

80

Make no moe offers, use no farther means,
But with all brief and plain conveniency
Let me have judgement, and the Jew his will.

Bassanio	For thy three thousand ducats here is six.
Shylock	If every ducat in six thousand ducats
	Were in six parts, and every part a ducat,
	I would not draw them; I would have my bond.
Duke	How shalt thou hope for mercy, rendering none?
Shylock	What judgement shall I dread, doing no wrong?
	You have among you many a purchas'd slave,

90

Which, like your asses, and your dogs, and mules,
You use in abject and in slavish parts,
Because you bought them. Shall I say to you,
Let them be free, marry them to your heirs?
Why sweat they under burthens? Let their beds
Be made as soft as yours, and let their palates
Be season'd with such viands? You will answer
"The slaves are ours": so do I answer you:
The pound of flesh which I demand of him
Is dearly bought, is mine and I will have it.

100

If you deny me, fie upon your law,
There is no force in the decrees of Venice.
I stand for judgement: answer, shall I have it?

Duke	Upon my power I may dismiss this court,
	Unless Bellario, a learnèd doctor,

---

77 **fretten:** chafed, rubbed
81 **moe:** more
102 **force:** authority

Bassanio to Shylock:
    "For thy three thousand ducats here is six."

	Whom I have sent for to determine this,	
	Come here to-day.	
Salerio	My lord, here stays without	
	A messenger with letters from the doctor,	
	New come from Padua.	
Duke	Bring us the letters, call the messenger.	110
Bassanio	Good cheer, Antonio! What, man, courage yet!	
	The Jew shall have my flesh, blood, bones and all,	
	Ere thou shalt lose for me one drop of blood.	
Antonio	I am a tainted wether of the flock,	
	Meetest for death; the weakest kind of fruit	
	Drops earliest to the ground, and so let me:	
	You cannot better be employ'd, Bassanio,	
	Than to live still, and write mine epitaph.	

Enter Nerissa, dressed like a lawyer's clerk

Duke	Came you from Padua, from Bellario?	
Nerissa	From both, my lord. Bellario greets your Grace.	120

Presenting a letter

Bassanio	Why dost thou whet thy knife so earnestly?	
Shylock	To cut the forfeiture from that bankrupt there.	
Gratiano	Not on thy sole, but on thy soul, harsh Jew.	
	Thou mak'st thy knife keen; but no metal can,	
	No, not the hangman's axe, bear half the keenness	
	Of thy sharp envy. Can no prayers pierce thee?	
Shylock	No, none that thou hast wit enough to make.	
Gratiano	O, be thou damn'd, inexecrable dog,	
	And for thy life let justice be accus'd!	
	Thou almost mak'st me waver in my faith,	130
	To hold opinion with Pythagoras,	
	That souls of animals infuse themselves	
	Into the trunks of men: thy currish spirit	[133–37]
	Govern'd a Wolf, who hang'd for human slaughter,	
	Even from the gallows did his fell soul fleet,	
	And, whilst thou lay'st in thy unhallow'd dam,	
	Infus'd itself in thee; for thy desires	
	Are wolvish, bloody, starv'd, and ravenous.	
Shylock	Till thou canst rail the seal from off my bond,	
	Thou but offend'st thy lungs to speak so loud:	140
	Repair thy wit, good youth, or it will fall	
	To cureless ruin. I stand here for law.	
Duke	This letter from Bellario doth commend	
	A young and learnèd doctor to our court:	
	Where is he?	

114	**tainted:** diseased	135 **fell:** fierce
	wether: ram	140 **offend'st:** strain

Nerissa	He attendeth here hard by,
	To know your answer, whether you'll admit him.
Duke	With all my heart: some three or four of you
	Go give him courteous conduct to this place;
	Meantime the court shall hear Bellario's letter.
	(*reads*) "Your Grace shall understand that at the
	receipt of your letter I am very sick, but in the instant
	that your messenger came, in loving visitation was
	with me a young doctor of Rome, his name is Bal-
	thasar. I acquainted him with the cause in contro-
	versy between the Jew and Antonio the merchant;
	we turn'd o'er many books together, he is furnish'd
	with my opinion, which, bettered with his own
	learning, the greatness whereof I cannot enough
	commend, comes with him at my importunity, to
	fill up your Grace's request in my stead. I beseech
	you, let his lack of years be no impediment to let
	him lack a reverend estimation, for I never knew so
	young a body with so old a head. I leave him to
	your gracious acceptance, whose trial shall better
	publish his commendation."
	You hear the learn'd Bellario, what he writes,
	And here, I take it, is the doctor come.

Enter Portia for Balthasar

	Give me your hand; come you from old Bellario?
Portia	I did, my lord.
Duke	You are welcome, take your place:
	Are you acquainted with the difference
	That holds this present question in the court?
Portia	I am informèd throughly of the cause;
	Which is the merchant here? And which the Jew?
Duke	Antonio and old Shylock, both stand forth.
Portia	Is your name Shylock?
Shylock	Shylock is my name.
Portia	Of a strange nature is the suit you follow,
	Yet in such rule, that the Venetian law
	Cannot impugn you as you do proceed.
	You stand within his danger, do you not?
Antonio	Ay, so he says.
Portia	Do you confess the bond?
Antonio	I do.
Portia	Then must the Jew be merciful.
Shylock	On what compulsion must I, tell me that.

Line numbers: 150, 160, 170, 180

---

178   **impugn:** question, challenge
179   **danger:** power

Portia	The quality of mercy is not strain'd,
	It droppeth as the gentle rain from heaven
	Upon the place beneath: it is twice blest,
	It blesseth him that gives, and him that takes;
	'Tis mightiest in the mightiest, it becomes
	The thronèd monarch better than his crown;
	His sceptre shows the force of temporal power,
	The attribute to awe and majesty, 190
	Wherein doth sit the dread and fear of kings;
	But mercy is above this sceptred sway,
	It is enthroned in the hearts of kings,
	It is an attribute to God himself;
	And earthly power doth then show likest God's
	When mercy seasons justice. Therefore, Jew,
	Though justice be thy plea, consider this,
	That, in the course of justice, none of us
	Should see salvation: we do pray for mercy,
	And that same prayer doth teach us all to render 200
	The deeds of mercy. I have spoke thus much
	To mitigate the justice of thy plea,
	Which if thou follow, this strict court of Venice
	Must needs give sentence 'gainst the merchant there.
Shylock	My deeds upon my head! I crave the law;
	The penalty and forfeit of my bond.
Portia	Is he not able to discharge the money?
Bassanio	Yes, here I tender it for him in the court,
	Yea, twice the sum, if that will not suffice,
	I will be bound to pay it ten times o'er, 210
	On forfeit of my hands, my head, my heart:
	If this will not suffice, it must appear
	That malice bears down truth. And I beseech you,
	Wrest once the law to your authority,
	To do a great right, do a little wrong,
	And curb this cruel devil of his will.
Portia	It must not be; there is no power in Venice
	Can alter a decree establishèd:
	'Twill be recorded for a precedent,
	And many an error by the same example 220
	Will rush into the state: it cannot be.
Shylock	A Daniel come to judgement! Yea, a Daniel!
	O wise young judge, how I do honour thee!
Portia	I pray you, let me look upon the bond.
Shylock	Here 'tis, most reverend doctor, here it is.
Portia	Shylock, there's thrice thy money offer'd thee.
Shylock	An oath, an oath, I have an oath in heaven:
	Shall I lay perjury upon my soul?
	No, not for Venice.

Portia · cour

Portia	Why, this bond is forfeit,
	And lawfully by this the Jew may claim 230
	A pound of flesh, to be by him cut off
	Nearest the merchant's heart. Be merciful,
	Take thrice thy money, bid me tear the bond.
Shylock	When it is paid according to the tenour.
	It doth appear you are a worthy judge,
	You know the law, your exposition
	Hath been most sound: I charge you by the law,
	Whereof you are a well-deserving pillar,
	Proceed to judgement: by my soul I swear,
	There is no power in the tongue of man 240
	To alter me: I stay here on my bond.
Antonio	Most heartily I do beseech the court
	To give the judgement.
Portia	Why then, thus it is;
	You must prepare your bosom for his knife.
Shylock	O noble judge! O excellent young man!
Portia	For the intent and purpose of the law
	Hath full relation to the penalty,
	Which here appeareth due upon the bond.
Shylock	'Tis very true: O wise and upright judge,
	How much more elder art thou than thy looks! 250
Portia	Therefore lay bare your bosom.
Shylock	Ay, his breast,
	So says the bond, doth it not, noble judge?
	"Nearest his heart," those are the very words.
Portia	It is so. Are there balance here to weigh
	The flesh?
Shylock	I have them ready.
Portia	Have by some surgeon, Shylock, on your charge,
	To stop his wounds, lest he do bleed to death.
Shylock	Is it so nominated in the bond?
Portia	It is not so express'd, but what of that?
	'Twere good you do so much for charity. 260
Shylock	I cannot find it, 'tis not in the bond.
Portia	You, merchant, have you any thing to say?
Antonio	But little: I am arm'd and well prepar'd;
	Give me your hand, Bassanio, fare you well,
	Grieve not that I am fallen to this for you;
	For herein Fortune shows herself more kind
	Than is her custom: it is still her use
	To let the wretched man outlive his wealth,
	To view with hollow eye and wrinkled brow

---

234 **tenour:** meaning of the document

	An age of poverty; from which lingering penance	270
	Of such misery doth she cut me off.	
	Commend me to your honourable wife,	
	Tell her the process of Antonio's end,	
	Say how I lov'd you, speak me fair in death;	
	And when the tale is told, bid her be judge	
	Whether Bassanio had not once a love.	
	Repent but you that you shall lose your friend,	
	And he repents not that he pays your debt;	
	For if the Jew do cut but deep enough,	
	I'll pay it instantly with all my heart.	280
Bassanio	Antonio, I am married to a wife	
	Which is as dear to me as life itself,	
	But life itself, my wife, and all the world,	
	Are not with me esteem'd above thy life:	
	I would lose all, ay, sacrifice them all	
	Here to this devil, to deliver you.	
Portia	Your wife would give you little thanks for that,	
	If she were by to hear you make the offer.	
Gratiano	I have a wife, who I protest I love;	
	I would she were in heaven, so she could	290
	Entreat some power to change this currish Jew.	
Nerissa	'Tis well you offer it behind her back,	
	The wish would make else an unquiet house.	
Shylock	These be the Christian husbands; I have a daughter;	
	Would any of the stock of Barrabas	
	Had been her husband rather than a Christian!	
	We trifle time, I pray thee pursue sentence.	
Portia	A pound of that same merchant's flesh is thine,	
	The court awards it, and the law doth give it.	
Shylock	Most rightful judge!	300
Portia	And you must cut this flesh from off his breast;	
	The law allows it, and the court awards it.	
Shylock	Most learnèd judge, a sentence! Come, prepare!	
Portia	Tarry a little; there is something else.	
	This bond doth give thee here no jot of blood,	
	The words expressly are "a pound of flesh":	
	Take then thy bond, take thou thy pound of flesh,	
	But in the cutting it, if thou dost shed	
	One drop of Christian blood, thy lands and goods	
	Are by the laws of Venice confiscate	310
	Unto the state of Venice.	
Gratiano	O upright judge! Mark, Jew: O learnèd judge!	
Shylock	Is that the law?	

---

273 **process:** story   282 **Which:** Who

Portia to Shylock as Antonio and his friends listen:
"And you must cut this flesh from off his breast;
The law allows it, and the court awards it.
Shylock: "Most learnèd judge, a sentence! Come, prepare!"

Portia	Thyself shalt see the act:
	For, as thou urgest justice, be assur'd
	Thou shalt have justice more than thou desirest.
Gratiano	O learnèd judge! Mark, Jew: a learnèd judge!
Shylock	I take this offer then, pay the bond thrice
	And let the Christian go.
Bassanio	Here is the money.
Portia	Soft!
	The Jew shall have all justice. Soft! No haste: 320
	He shall have nothing but the penalty.
Gratiano	O Jew! An upright judge, a learnèd judge!
Portia	Therefore prepare thee to cut off the flesh.
	Shed thou no blood, nor cut thou less nor more
	But just a pound of flesh: if thou tak'st more
	Or less than a just pound, be it but so much
	As makes it light or heavy in the substance,
	Or the division of the twentieth part
	Of one poor scruple; nay, if the scale do turn
	But in the estimation of a hair, 330
	Thou diest, and all thy goods are confiscate.
Gratiano	A second Daniel, a Daniel, Jew!
	Now, infidel, I have you on the hip.
Portia	Why doth the Jew pause? Take thy forfeiture.
Shylock	Give me my principal, and let me go.
Bassanio	I have it ready for thee, here it is.
Portia	He hath refus'd it in the open court,
	He shall have merely justice and his bond.
Gratiano	A Daniel, still say I, a second Daniel!
	I thank thee, Jew for teaching me that word. 340
Shylock	Shall I not have barely my principal?
Portia	Thou shalt have nothing but the forfeiture,
	To be so taken at thy peril, Jew.
Shylock	Why, then the devil give him good of it!
	I'll stay no longer question.
Portia	Tarry, Jew,
	The law hath yet another hold on you.
	It is enacted in the laws of Venice,
	If it be prov'd against an alien
	That by direct or indirect attempts
	He seek the life of any citizen, 350
	The party 'gainst the which he doth contrive
	Shall seize one half his goods, the other half
	Comes to the privy coffer of the state,

325 **just:** exact
329 **scruple:** small weight
348 **alien:** Jews could not become citizens

	And the offender's life lies in the mercy
	Of the Duke only, 'gainst all other voice.
	In which predicament I say thou stand'st;
	For it appears, by manifest proceeding,
	That indirectly, and directly too,
	Thou hast contriv'd against the very life
	Of the defendant; and thou hast incurr'd
	The danger formerly by me rehears'd.
	Down therefore, and beg mercy of the Duke.
Gratiano	Beg that thou mayst have leave to hang thyself:
	And yet, thy wealth being forfeit to the state,
	Thou hast not left the value of a cord;
	Therefore thou must be hang'd at the state's charge.
Duke	That thou shalt see the difference of our spirit,
	I pardon thee thy life before you ask it:
	For half thy wealth, it is Antonio's,
	The other half comes to the general state,
	Which humbleness may drive unto a fine.
Portia	Ay, for the state, not for Antonio.
Shylock	Nay, take my life and all, pardon not that:
	You take my house, when you do take the prop
	That doth sustain my house; you take my life,
	When you do take the means whereby I live.
Portia	What mercy can you render him, Antonio?
Gratiano	A halter gratis, nothing else for God's sake.
Antonio	So please my lord the Duke, and all the court,
	To quit the fine for one half of his goods,
	I am content; so he will let me have
	The other half in use, to render it,
	Upon his death, unto the gentleman
	That lately stole his daughter:
	Two things provided more, that, for this favour,
	He presently become a Christian:
	The other, that he do record a gift,
	Here in the court, of all he dies possess'd,
	Unto his son Lorenzo and his daughter.
Duke	He shall do this, or else I do recant
	The pardon that I late pronounced here.
Portia	Art thou contented, Jew? What dost thou say?
Shylock	I am content.
Portia	Clerk, draw a deed of gift.
Shylock	I pray you, give me leave to go from hence;
	I am not well, send the deed after me,
	And I will sign it.

Line numbers in right margin: 360, 370, 380, 390.

---

380 **quit:** cancel
382 **use:** trust

Shylock:
"Nay, take my life and all, pardon not that:
You take my house, when you do take the prop
That doth sustain my house; you take my life
When you do take the means whereby I live."

Duke	Get thee gone, but do it.
Gratiano	In christening shalt thou have two godfathers:
	Had I been judge, thou shouldst have had ten more,
	To bring thee to the gallows, not the font.

Exit Shylock

Duke	Sir, I entreat you home with me to dinner.	400
Portia	I humbly do desire your Grace of pardon,	
	I must away this night toward Padua,	
	And it is meet I presently set forth.	
Duke	I am sorry that your leisure serves you not.	
	Antonio, gratify this gentleman,	
	For, in my mind, you are much bound to him.	

Exit Duke and his train

Bassanio	Most worthy gentleman, I and my friend	
	Have by your wisdom been this day acquitted	
	Of grievous penalties, in lieu whereof,	
	Three thousand ducats, due unto the Jew,	410
	We freely cope your courteous pains withal.	
Antonio	And stand indebted, over and above,	
	In love and service to you evermore.	
Portia	He is well paid that is well satisfied,	
	And I, delivering you, am satisfied,	
	And therein do account myself well paid;	
	My mind was never yet more mercenary.	
	I pray you, know me when we meet again,	
	I wish you well, and so I take my leave.	
Bassanio	Dear sir, of force I must attempt you further;	420
	Take some remembrance of us as a tribute,	
	Not as a fee: grant me two things, I pray you,	
	Not to deny me, and to pardon me.	
Portia	You press me far, and therefore I will yield.	
	Give me your gloves, I'll wear them for your sake;	
	And, for your love, I'll take this ring from you:	
	Do not draw back your hand, I'll take no more,	
	And you in love shall not deny me this.	
Bassanio	This ring, good sir, alas, is a trifle!	
	I will not shame myself to give you this.	430
Portia	I will have nothing else but only this,	
	And now methinks I have a mind to it.	
Bassanio	There's more depends on this than on the value.	
	The dearest ring in Venice will I give you,	

398 **ten more:** i.e., a jury
399 **font:** basin holding the baptismal water
405 **gratify:** reward
411 **cope:** match
420 **attempt:** persuade

Nerissa to Portia:
  "I'll see if I can get my husband's ring,
  Which I did make him swear to keep for ever."

<table>
<tr><td></td><td>And find it out by proclamation,
Only for this I pray you pardon me.</td><td></td></tr>
<tr><td>**Portia**</td><td>I see, sir, you are liberal in offers;
You taught me first to beg, and now methinks
You teach me how a beggar should be answer'd.</td><td></td></tr>
<tr><td>**Bassanio**</td><td>Good sir, this ring was given me by my wife,
And when she put it on, she made me vow
That I should neither sell, nor give, nor lose it.</td><td>440</td></tr>
<tr><td>**Portia**</td><td>That 'scuse serves many men to save their gifts;
And if your wife be not a mad woman,
And know how well I have deserv'd this ring,
She would not hold out enemy for ever
For giving it to me. Well, peace be with you!</td><td></td></tr>
</table>

Exeunt Portia and Nerissa

Antonio	My Lord Bassanio, let him have the ring, Let his deservings and my love withal Be valued 'gainst your wife's commandment.	450
Bassanio	Go, Gratiano, run and overtake him, Give him the ring, and bring him, if thou canst, Unto Antonio's house. Away! Make haste.	

Exit Gratiano

Come, you and I will thither presently,
And in the morning early will we both
Fly toward Belmont: come, Antonio.   *Exeunt*

Scene 2

The same. A street

Enter Portia and Nerissa

Portia	Inquire the Jew's house out, give him this deed, And let him sign it: we'll away to-night, And be a day before our husbands home: This deed will be well welcome to Lorenzo.

Enter Gratiano

Gratiano	Fair sir, you are well o'erta'en: My Lord Bassanio upon more advice

---

443 **'scuse:** excuse
  5 **well:** fortunately
  6 **advice:** consideration, discussion

	Hath sent you here this ring, and doth entreat
	Your company at dinner.
Portia	That cannot be:
	His ring I do accept most thankfully:
	And so I pray you tell him: furthermore,
	I pray you show my youth old Shylock's house.
Gratiano	That I will do.
Nerissa	Sir, I would speak with you.
	(*aside to Portia*) I'll see if I can get my husband's ring,
	Which I did make him swear to keep for ever.
Portia	(*aside to Nerissa*) Thou mayst, I warrant. We shall
	have old swearing
	That they did give the rings away to men;
	But we'll outface them, and outswear them too.
	(*aloud*) Away! Make haste: thou know'st where I
	will tarry.
Nerissa	Come, good sir, will you show me to this house?

10

Exeunt

---

15   **old:** rare

Act Fifth

Scene 1

[Scene 20]

Belmont. Avenue to Portia's house

Enter Lorenzo and Jessica

Lorenzo The moon shines bright: in such a night as this,   [1–14]
When the sweet wind did gently kiss the trees,
And they did make no noise, in such a night
Troilus methinks mounted the Troyan walls,
And sigh'd his soul toward the Grecian tents,
Where Cressid lay that night.

Jessica   In such a night
Did Thisbe fearfully o'ertrip the dew,
And saw the lion's shadow ere himself,
And ran dismay'd away.

Lorenzo   In such a night
Stood Dido with a willow in her hand   10
Upon the wild sea banks, and waft her love
To come again to Carthage.

Jessica   In such a night
Medea gather'd the enchanted herbs
That did renew old Aeson.

Lorenzo   In such a night
Did Jessica steal from the wealthy Jew,
And with an unthrift love did run from Venice,
As far as Belmont.

Jessica   In such a night
Did young Lorenzo swear he lov'd her well,

---

4 **Troilus:** a Trojan prince
6 **Cressid:** Cressida, a Greek maiden, beloved of Troilus
7 **Thisbe:** a beautiful Babylonian maiden
10 **Dido:** Queen of Carthage
13 **Medea:** wife of Jason

100

Lorenzo to Jessica:
   "In such a night
   Did Jessica steal from a wealthy Jew,
   And with an unthrift love did run from Venice . . ."

	Stealing her soul with many vows of faith,	
	And ne'er a true one.	
Lorenzo	In such a night	20
	Did pretty Jessica, like a little shrew,	
	Slander her love, and he forgave it her.	
Jessica	I would out-night you, did no body come;	
	But, hark, I hear the footing of a man.	

Enter Stephano

Lorenzo	Who comes so fast in silence of the night?	
Stephano	A friend.	
Lorenzo	A friend! What friend? Your name, I pray you,	[27]
	friend?	
Stephano	Stephano is my name, and I bring word	
	My mistress will before the break of day	
	Be here at Belmont: she doth stray about	30
	By holy crosses, where she kneels and prays	
	For happy wedlock hours.	
Lorenzo	Who comes with her?	
Stephano	None but a holy hermit and her maid.	
	I pray you, is my master yet return'd?	
Lorenzo	He is not, nor we have not heard from him.	
	But go we in, I pray thee, Jessica,	
	And ceremoniously let us prepare	
	Some welcome for the mistress of the house.	

Enter Launcelot

Launcelot	Sola, sola! Wo ha, ho! Sola, sola!	
Lorenzo	Who calls?	40
Launcelot	Sola! Did you see Master Lorenzo? Master Lorenzo,	
	sola, sola!	
Lorenzo	Leave hollaing, man: here.	
Launcelot	Sola! Where? Where?	
Lorenzo	Here.	
Launcelot	Tell him there's a post come from my master, with	
	his horn full of good news: my master will be here	
	ere morning. *Exit*	
Lorenzo	Sweet soul, let's in, and there expect their coming.	
	And yet no matter: why should we go in?	50
	My friend Stephano, signify, I pray you,	
	Within the house, your mistress is at hand,	
	And bring your music forth into the air.	
	Exit Stephano	
	How sweet the moonlight sleeps upon this bank!	

---

39 **Sola:** a hunting cry
46 **post:** messenger

Here will we sit, and let the sounds of music
Creep in our ears: soft stillness and the night
Become the touches of sweet harmony.
Sit, Jessica; look how the floor of heaven
Is thick inlaid with patens of bright gold;
There's not the smallest orb which thou behold'st   60
But in his motion like an angel sings,
Still quiring to the young-eyed cherubins;
Such harmony is in immortal souls,
But whilst this muddy vesture of decay
Doth grossly close it in, we cannot hear it.

Enter Musicians

Come, ho, and wake Diana with a hymn!
With sweetest touches pierce your mistress' ear,
And draw her home with music.   *Music*

Jessica   I am never merry when I hear sweet music.
Lorenzo   The reason is, your spirits are attentive: 70
For do but note a wild and wanton herd,
Or race of youthful and unhandled colts,
Fetching mad bounds, bellowing and neighing loud,
Which is the hot condition of their blood;
If they but hear perchance a trumpet sound,
Or any air of music touch their ears,
You shall perceive them make a mutual stand,
Their savage eyes turn'd to a modest gaze,
By the sweet power of music: therefore the poet
Did feign that Orpheus drew trees, stones, and floods;   80
Since nought so stockish, hard, and full of rage,
But music for the time doth change his nature;
The man that hath no music in himself,
Nor is not mov'd with concord of sweet sounds,
Is fit for treasons, stratagems, and spoils;
The motions of his spirit are dull as night,
And his affections dark as Erebus:
Let no such man be trusted. Mark the music.

Enter Portia and Nerissa

Portia   That light we see is burning in my hall:
How far that little candle throws his beams!   90
So shines a good deed in a naughty world.
Nerissa   When the moon shone we did not see the candle.
Portia   So doth the greater glory dim the less;
A substitute shines brightly as a king,

---

57 **touches:** notes
59 **paten:** small flat dish
62 **quiring:** singing (from choir)
66 **Diana:** goddess of the moon

79 **the poet:** (Ovid)
80 **Orpheus:** a divinely inspired musician
87 **Erebus:** dark place on the way to Hades

	Until a king be by, and then his state	
	Empties itself, as doth an inland brook	
	Into the main of waters. Music! Hark!	
Nerissa	It is your music, madam, of the house.	
Portia	Nothing is good, I see, with respect:	
	Methinks it sounds much sweeter than by day.	100
Nerissa	Silence bestows that virtue on it, madam.	
Portia	The crow doth sing as sweetly as the lark,	
	When neither is attended; and I think	
	The nightingale, if she should sing by day,	
	When every goose is cackling, would be thought	
	No better a musician than the wren.	
	How many things by season season'd are	
	To their right praise, and true perfection!	
	Peace, how the moon sleeps with Endymion,	
	And would not be awak'd. *Music ceases*	
Lorenzo	That is the voice,	110
	Or I am much deceiv'd, of Portia.	
Portia	He knows me as the blind man knows the cuckoo,	
	By the bad voice.	
Lorenzo	Dear lady, welcome home.	
Portia	We have been praying for our husbands' welfare,	
	Which speed, we hope, the better for our words:	
	Are they return'd?	
Lorenzo	Madam, they are not yet;	
	But there is come a messenger before,	
	To signify their coming.	
Portia	Go in, Nerissa;	
	Give order to my servants that they take	
	No note at all of our being absent hence,	120
	Nor you Lorenzo, Jessica nor you.	
	A tucket sounds	
Lorenzo	Your husband is at hand, I hear his trumpet;	
	We are no tell-tales, madam, fear you not.	
Portia	This night methinks is but the daylight sick;	
	It looks a little paler: 'tis a day,	
	Such as the day is when the sun is hid.	

Enter Bassanio, Antonio, Gratiano, and their followers

Bassanio	We should hold day with the Antipodes,	
	If you would walk in absence of the sun.	
Portia	Let me give light, but let me not be light,	

103 **neither is attended:** either is alone
109 **Endymion:** (i.e., Lorenzo): a youth beloved by Diana, (i.e., Jessica)
who put him into an eternal sleep to preserve his youth
121 **tucket:** flourish

Bassanio
'The Merchant
of Venice'
Stratford 1984

C. Poddubiuk

	For a light wife doth make a heavy husband,	130
	And never be Bassanio so for me:	
	But God sort all! You are welcome home, my lord.	
Bassanio	I thank you, madam; give welcome to my friend.	
	This is the man, this is Antonio,	
	To whom I am so infinitely bound.	
Portia	You should in all sense be much bound to him,	
	For, as I hear, he was much bound for you.	
Antonio	No more than I am well acquitted of.	
Portia	Sir, you are very welcome to our house:	
	It must appear in other ways than words,	140
	Therefore I scant this breathing courtesy,	
Gratiano	(*to Nerissa*) By yonder moon I swear you do me	
	wrong;	
	In faith, I gave it to the judge's clerk;	
	Would he were gelt that had it, for my part,	
	Since you do take it, love, so much at heart.	
Portia	A quarrel, ho, already! What's the matter?	
Gratiano	About a hoop of gold, a paltry ring	
	That she did give me, whose posy was	
	For all the world like cutler's poetry	
	Upon a knife, "Love me, and leave me not."	150
Nerissa	What talk you of the posy or the value?	
	You swore to me when I did give it you,	
	That you would wear it till your hour of death,	
	And that it should lie with you in your grave:	
	Though not for me, yet for your vehement oaths,	
	You should have been respective and have kept it.	
	Gave it a judge's clerk! No, God's my judge,	
	The clerk will ne'er wear hair on 's face that had it.	
Gratiano	He will, an if he live to be a man.	
Nerissa	Ay, if a woman live to be a man.	160
Gratiano	Now, by this hand, I gave it to a youth,	
	A kind of boy, a little scrubbèd boy,	
	No higher than thyself, the judge's clerk,	
	A prating boy, that begg'd it as a fee:	
	I could not for my heart deny it him.	
Portia	You were to blame, I must be plain with you,	
	To part so slightly with your wife's first gift,	
	A thing stuck on with oaths upon your finger,	
	And so riveted with faith unto your flesh.	
	I gave my love a ring, and made him swear	170

130	**light:** frivolous, unfaithful	148	**posy:** motto (engraved)
141	**scant:** cut short	156	**respective:** respectful
143	**gelt:** gelded	162	**scrubbèd:** scrubby

	Never to part with it, and here he stands;
	I dare be sworn for him he would not leave it,
	Nor pluck it from his finger, for the wealth
	That the world masters. Now, in faith, Gratiano,
	You give your wife too unkind a cause of grief:
	And 'twere to me, I should be mad at it.
Bassanio	(*aside*) Why, I were best to cut my left hand off,
	And swear I lost the ring defending it.
Gratiano	My Lord Bassanio gave his ring away
	Unto the judge that begg'd it, and indeed
	Deserv'd it too; and then the boy, his clerk,
	That took some pains in writing, he begg'd mine,
	And neither man not master would take aught
	But the two rings.
Portia	What ring gave you, my lord?
	Not that, I hope, which you receiv'd of me.
Bassanio	If I could add a lie unto a fault,
	I would deny it; but you see my finger
	Hath not the ring upon it; it is gone.
Portia	Even so void is your false heart of truth.
	By heaven, I will ne'er come in your bed
	Until I see the ring.
Nerissa	Nor I in yours
	Till I again see mine.
Bassanio	Sweet Portia,
	If you did know to whom I gave the ring,
	If you did know for whom I gave the ring,
	And would conceive for what I gave the ring,
	And how unwillingly I left the ring,
	When nought would be accepted but the ring,
	You would abate the strength of your displeasure.
Portia	If you had known the virtue of the ring,
	Or half her worthiness that gave the ring,
	Or your own honour to contain the ring,
	You would not then have parted with the ring.
	What man is there so much unreasonable,
	If you had pleas'd to have defended it
	With any terms of zeal, wanted the modesty
	To urge the thing held as a ceremony?
	Nerissa teaches me what to believe;
	I'll die for 't but some woman had the ring.
Bassanio	No, by my honour, madam, by my soul.

180

190

200

---

174 **masters:** possesses
206 **urge:** demand **ceremony:** token

	No woman had it, but a civil doctor,	210
	Which did refuse three thousand ducats of me,	
	And begg'd the ring, the which I did deny him,	
	And suffer'd him to go displeas'd away;	
	Even he that had held up the very life	
	Of my dear friend. What should I say, sweet lady?	
	I was enforc'd to send it after him,	
	I was beset with shame and courtesy,	
	My honour would not let ingratitude	
	So much besmear it. Pardon me, good lady,	
	For by these blessed candles of the night,	220
	Had you been there, I think you would have begg'd	
	The ring of me to give the worthy doctor.	
Portia	Let not that doctor e'er come near my house,	
	Since he hath got the jewel that I lov'd,	
	And that which you did swear to keep for me,	
	I will become as liberal as you;	
	I'll not deny him any thing I have,	
	No, not my body nor my husband's bed;	
	Know him I shall, I am well sure of it:	
	Lie not a night from home; watch me like Argus;	230
	If you do not, if I be left alone,	
	Now, by mine honour, which is yet mine own,	
	I'll have that doctor for my bedfellow.	
Nerissa	And I his clerk; therefore be well advis'd	
	How you do leave me to mine own protection.	
Gratiano	Well, do you so: let not me take him then,	
	For if I do, I'll mar the young clerk's pen.	
Antonio	I am the unhappy subject of these quarrels.	
Portia	Sir, grieve not you, you are welcome notwithstanding.	
Bassanio	Portia, forgive me this enforcèd wrong,	240
	And, in the hearing of these many friends,	
	I swear to thee, even by thine own fair eyes,	
	Wherein I see myself, –	
Portia	Mark you but that!	
	In both my eyes he doubly sees himself;	
	In each eye one: swear by your double self,	
	And there's an oath of credit.	
Bassanio	Nay, but hear me:	
	Pardon this fault, and by my soul I swear	
	I never more will break an oath with thee.	

---

217 **courtesy:** a sense of obligation
230 **Argus:** the hundred-eyed watchman of Greek myth
236 **take:** catch

Antonio	I once did lend my body for his wealth,
	Which, but for him that had your husband's ring, 250
	Had quite miscarried: I dare be bound again,
	My soul upon the forfeit, that your lord
	Will never more break faith advisèdly.
Portia	Then you shall be his surety. Give him this,
	And bid him keep it better than the other.
Antonio	Here, Lord Bassanio, swear to keep this ring.
Bassanio	By heaven, it is the same I gave the doctor!
Portia	I had it of him: pardon me, Bassanio,
	For, by this ring, the doctor lay with me.
Nerissa	And pardon me, my gentle Gratiano, 260
	For that same scrubbèd boy, the doctor's clerk,
	In lieu of this last night did lie with me.
Gratiano	Why, this is like the mending of highways
	In summer, where the ways are fair enough:
	What, are we cuckolds ere we have deserv'd it?
Portia	Speak not so grossly. You are all amaz'd:
	Here is a letter, read it at your leisure,
	It comes from Padua, from Bellario:
	There you shall find that Portia was the doctor,
	Nerissa there her clerk: Lorenzo here 270
	Shall witness I set forth as soon as you,
	And even but now return'd; I have not yet
	Enter'd my house. Antonio, you are welcome,
	And I have better news in store for you
	Than you expect: unseal this letter soon;
	There you shall find three of your argosies
	Are richly come to harbour suddenly:
	You shall not know by what strange accident
	I chanced on this letter.
Antonio	I am dumb.
Bassanio	Were you the doctor, and I knew you not? 280
Gratiano	Were you the clerk that is to make me cuckold?
Nerissa	Ay, but the clerk that never means to do it,
	Unless he live until he be a man.
Bassanio	Sweet doctor, you shall be my bedfellow;
	When I am absent, then lie with my wife.
Antonio	Sweet lady, you have given me life and living;
	For here I read for certain that my ships
	Are safely come to road.

---

253 **advisedly:** consciously
262 **In lieu of:** In return of
265 **cuckolds:** husbands of unfaithful wives
288 **road:** harbour

Portia	How now, Lorenzo?
	My clerk hath some good comforts too for you.
Nerissa	Ay, and I'll give them him without a fee.
	There do I give to you and Jessica,
	From the rich Jew, a special deed of gift,
	After his death, of all he dies possess'd of.
Lorenzo	Fair ladies, you drop manna in the way
	Of starved people.
Portia	It is almost morning,
	And yet I am sure you are not satisfied
	Of these events at full. Let us go in,
	And charge us there upon inter'gatories,
	And we will answer all things faithfully.
Gratiano	Let it be so, the first inter'gatory
	That my Nerissa shall be sworn on, is,
	Whether till the next night she had rather stay
	Or go to bed now, being two hours to day:
	But were the day come, I should wish it dark,
	That I were couching with the doctor's clerk.
	Well, while I live, I'll fear no other thing
	So sore, as keeping safe Nerissa's ring. *Exeunt*

290

300

---

298   **charge us there upon inter'gatories:** demand answers under oath
      to cross-questioning

Gratiano:
   "Well, while I live, I'll fear no other thing
   So sore, as keeping safe Nerissa's ring."

**Old Gobbo and Launcelot surrounded by the
Punchinellos.**

Stratford Festival Edition Emendations

In the 1984 Stratford Festival Production of *The Merchant of Venice*, the following changes were made in the text for various reasons. Occasionally a new word was interjected in order to complement the action of a scene, or an obscure word was changed to a more accessible equivalent. In both cases, anachronism was avoided by using a word that would have been in use in Shakespeare's time.

Often entire lines were cut. Although their meaning was clear to the actor or to someone reading the words on the page with the aid of a glossary, it was found that certain opaque references interfered with the action of the play.

Often, lines are cut before the first rehearsal. As the creative process continues, many actors discover that certain lines are essential to the emotional through-line of the characters they are playing, and the lines are reinstated. Therefore, certain emendations listed here are suggested cuts that were reinstated during rehearsals or even after the official opening night.

Some of the more difficult lines spoken in the play have been paraphrased as an aid to readers.

Although such liberties may startle the purist, they ultimately lead to a greater enjoyment of the play on the part of the general audience.

Act I / Scene 1

lines 50–56: "Now by two-headed Janus . . . be laughable." These lines were cut to expedite the action of the scene. *Janus* was the Roman god of peace and war, represented with two heads. *Nestor* was the wisest and therefore gravest of the Greeks.

lines 101–102: "But fish not . . . this opinion." These lines were cut. *Gudgeon* is a small fish.

Act I / Scene 2

line 8: *superfluity* was changed to *extravagance*.

line 9: *competency* was changed to *moderation*.

lines 61–63: "if he would . . . requite him." These lines were cut.

lines 68–69: "and you will . . . in the English." These lines were cut. *come into the court* could mean *bear me witness*.

| lines 71–80: | "How oddly . . . for another." These lines were cut. *Scottish Lord* may have been changed to *other Lord* in deference to King James. |
| line 119: | "the four suitors." As many critics have noted, in fact six suitors have been mentioned. Presumably the English and Scottish lords were added at a later date. |

Act I /Scene 3

line 15:	*supposition* was changed to *doubt*.
lines 66–85:	This is a story from the Bible. (See Genesis 30: 31–43.)
line 73:	*compromis'd* was changed to *then agreed*.

Act II / Scene 1

| lines 31–38: | "But alas the while . . . die with grieving." These lines were cut. Lichas was Hercules' servant. |

Act II / Scene 2

| lines 150–159: | "Father, in . . . simple scapes. Well," These lines were cut to expedite the action of the scene. |
| line 160: | *gear* was changed to *business*. |

Act II / Scene 5

| lines 23–27: | "but if you do . . . in the afternoon." These obscure lines were cut to expedite the action of the scene. |

Act II / Scene 7

line 1:	"Go, draw . . . discover" was changed to "Pray discover you." Since the play was performed on a thrust stage, there was no curtain to draw and the caskets were therefore carried on.
lines 41–47:	"The Hyrcanian . . . fair Portia." These lines were cut. The Hyrcanian deserts are south of the Caspian Sea.
line 78:	"Draw the curtains" was changed to "Take the caskets."

Act II / Scene 8

| lines 27–34: | "I reason'd with . . . may grieve him." These lines were cut. |

**Stewart Robertson preparing the fool's head for the casket
chosen by the Prince of Arragon.**

The Merchant of Venice

Act II / *Scene 9*

lines 27–29: "Which pries not . . . of casualty." These lines were cut.

lines 62–64: "The fire . . . choose amiss." These lines were cut.

line 83: "draw the curtain" was changed to "bring the caskets."

Act III / *Scene 1*

lines 8–10: "I would she . . . a third husband." These lines were cut to expedite the action of the scene.

line 99: *Here in Genoa* is clearly wrong. It is frequently emended to *Where? In Genoa?* It has also been suggested that something is missing and the line might read "What other news didst hear in Genoa?"

Act III / *Scene 3*

lines 35: *God* was interjected between *pray* and *Bassanio*.

Act III / *Scene 4*

lines 68–76: "and speak of frays . . . a twelvemonth." These lines were cut.

Act III / *Scene 5*

line 22: *hogs* was changed to *pigs*.

lines 35–44: "I shall answer . . . parrots." These lines were cut to expedite the action of the scene.

lines 46–52: "Then bid them . . . wit in an instant." These lines were cut.

lines 60–65: "O dear discretion . . . Defy the matter." These lines were cut.

Act IV / *Scene 1*

lines 133–137: "thy currish spirit . . . itself in thee." These lines were cut. *a wolf* is a reference to Queen Elizabeth's Jewish physician, who was executed in England in June 1594. Since he was commonly known as *Lopus*, the reference to *Lupus* (wolf) is easy.

Act V / *Scene 1*

lines 1–14: Note the many references to classical lovers in this sequence, several of whom are common to other plays by Shakespeare: Troilus and Cressida, Thisbe (and Pyramus) of *A Midsummer Night's Dream*, and Dido and Aeneas, who are mentioned in *The Tempest*.

line 27: "A friend . . . friend?" this line was cut.

Biographical Notes

Mark Lamos

Mark Lamos makes his Stratford debut this season directing the Festival production of *The Merchant of Venice.*

After graduating from Northwestern University, where he majored in music, Mr. Lamos began his theatrical career as an actor. In 1978 he was appointed artistic director of the California Shakespearean Festival, and received international acclaim for productions of *Romeo and Juliet, The Taming of the Shrew, Hamlet,* and *A Midsummer Night's Dream.* For the Arizona Theatre Company he directed *A Flea in Her Ear, Twelfth Night, The Seagull,* and *The Show-off.* For Guthrie II in Minneapolis, he directed *Dear Liar* and Athol Fugard's *Hello and Good-bye.*

In 1977 Mr. Lamos became artistic director of Connecticut's Hartford Stage Company, where his productions have included *Cymbeline, As You Like It, Antony and Cleopatra,* Sartre's *Kean, The Greeks, The Misanthrope,* the U.S. première of Tom Stoppard's adaptation of Arthur Schnitzler's *Undiscovered Country,* and a commissioned translation by Lanford Wilson of *Three Sisters.* He also directed new productions of *Arabella* for Santa Fe Opera, *Don Giovanni* for Opera Theatre of St. Louis, and the world première of John Harbison's *Winter's Tale* for San Francisco Opera.

David Street

Christina Poddubiuk

Christina Poddubiuk returns to the Stratford Festival as designer for *The Merchant of Venice*. Previous Festival credits include designs for the 1983 Young Company production of *Much Ado About Nothing* and the 1982 Shakespeare 3 production of *All's Well That Ends Well*. She also worked as design assistant on *The Gondoliers*.

Ms. Poddubiuk was educated at McGill University and graduated from the National Theatre School in 1982.

Past credits include set and costume design for *Lady from the Sea* (Centaur Theatre, Montreal), two seasons with the Piggery Theatre in Quebec, and several productions of the Saidye Bronfman Theatre in Montreal and Les Productions d'Etoiles in New Brunswick.

Her most recent credits include costume design for *Chairs and Tables* (Tarragon Theatre), set and costume design for *The Jail Diary of Albie Sachs* (Toronto Workshop Productions), and costume design for *Toad of Toad Hall* (Centre Stage).

Ms. Poddubiuk is the recipient of a 1981 Tyrone Guthrie Award and a 1983 Tom Patterson Award.

Jane Edmonds

Elliott Hayes

Elliott Hayes is the Associate Literary Manager of the Stratford Festival. For the 1982 Festival Season he was Assistant Director of *Arms and the Man*, and editor and writer of additional material for *A Variable Passion*. In 1973 he was Assistant Director of *The Marriage Brokers* at Stratford. A Stratford native, Mr. Hayes trained for three years at the Bristol Old Vic Theatre School in England. He was co-director of *The Caucasian Chalk Circle* and *A Midsummer Night's Dream* for the Verde Valley School in Arizona. Mr. Hayes has staged readings of original poetry, and his play *Summer and Fall* was workshopped at Stratford in 1981. In the 1983 Stratford season his play, *Blake*, was presented on The Third Stage, with Douglas Campbell in the *tour-de-force* role. His novel *American Slang* is currently under option to be filmed. Mr. Hayes is co-editor of the Stratford Festival Editions.

David Street

Michal Schonberg

Michal Schonberg is the Literary Manager of the Stratford Festival. His responsibilities include all the literary matters of the theatre, contacts with playwrights, scholars, and lecturers, as well as consultation on repertory. He is also co-editor of the Stratford Festival Editions. Associate Professor of Drama and Co-ordinator of Drama Studies at Scarborough College, University of Toronto. Mr. Schonberg has translated several works from Czech into English. He has also translated two of Tom Stoppard's plays, *Every Good Boy Deserves Favour* and *Professional Foul*, into Czech. He co-edited John Hirsch's adaptation of *The Dybbuk*, for publication and has had several works and adaptations published in *World Literature Today* and *Modern Drama*. Mr. Schonberg prepared the 1982 Stratford version of *Mary Stuart* with translator Joe McClinton.

Stratford Festival Editions

The Tempest
directed by John Hirsch

Macbeth
directed by Des McAnuff

As You Like It
directed by John Hirsch

The Taming of the Shrew
directed by Peter Dews

The Merry Wives of Windsor
directed by Robert Beard

A Midsummer Night's Dream
directed by John Hirsch

Romeo and Juliet
directed by Peter Dews and Steven Schipper

The Merchant of Venice
directed by Mark Lamos

For more information, write to:
Stratford Festival Editions
CBC Enterprises
P.O. Box 500, Station A
Toronto, Canada M5W 1E6